1 CORINTHIANS

THE CHALLENGES OF LIFE TOGETHER

PAUL STEVENS
& DAN WILLIAMS

13 STUDIES
FOR INDIVIDUALS
OR GROUPS

INTER-VARSITY PRESS
36 Causton Street, London SW1P 4ST, England
Email: ivp@ivpbooks.com
Website: www.ivpbooks.com

Originally published in the United States of America in the LifeGuide® Bible Studies series
in 1988 by InterVarsity Press, Downers Grove, Illinois
Second edition published in 2001
First published in Great Britain by Scripture Union in 2001
Second UK edition published in 2017
This edition published in Great Britain by Inter-Varsity Press 2020

British Library Cataloguing-in-Publication Data
A catalogue record for this book is available from the British Library.

ISBN: 978-1-78359-858-8

Printed in Great Britain by Ashford Colour Press Ltd, Gosport, Hampshire

*Inter-Varsity Press publishes Christian books that are true to the Bible and that communicate
the gospel, develop discipleship and strengthen the church for its mission in the world.*

*IVP originated within the Inter-Varsity Fellowship, now the Universities and Colleges
Christian Fellowship, a student movement connecting Christian Unions in universities and
colleges throughout Great Britain, and a member movement of the International Fellowship of
Evangelical Students. Website: www.uccf.org.uk. That historic association is maintained,
and all senior IVP staff and committee members subscribe to the UCCF Basis of Faith.*

Contents

Getting the Most
Out of *1 Corinthians*

In 1938, just before World War II, Dietrich Bonhoeffer wrote *Life Together*, a moving little book on the principles of Christian community. Eighteen and a half centuries earlier the apostle Paul wrote what has come to be known as 1 Corinthians, a fascinating commentary on one Christian community that he founded. Why should we bother with either of these books?

Simply because we all have to live together with people, in Christian contexts and otherwise. Whether the situation involves a close friendship, a roommate, a spouse, a small group, a family, an office, a campus club, a neighborhood or a congregation, the challenges of life together will inevitably crop up. Church life is not immune to these problems, and Corinth was particularly susceptible. As a result, we can benefit from Paul's advice to that community.

Are there cliques and power struggles in the communities you are a part of? Are you plagued by people who think they are spiritually or intellectually superior? How do you handle the immorality that seems so prevalent in the world, especially when it begins to invade the church? What is the proper way to exercise your rights, especially when a friend wrongs you or you feel that a matter of principle is at stake? How do we regulate marriage and singleness in the face of so many attacks on the health of both these life situations? How are we ever going to solve the battle of the sexes? What is the path to respecting one another's personality and gifts? Can eternity make a difference in how we live together today? If any of these questions are relevant to your life and communities, then 1 Corinthians has something to say to you.

The relationship between Paul and the church at Corinth is a bittersweet chapter in church history. As the apostle traveled down the isthmus joining the two halves of Achaia (Greece) and first spotted the plain surrounding the city and the hill known as the Acrocorinth jutting up behind, he could hardly have imagined the depths and heights that would be reached by the church he left behind eighteen months later. (See Acts 18 for the background of this part of Paul's second missionary journey.) Nor could Paul have any idea of the depths and heights of emotion to which the members of that church would lead him, their spiritual father, over the next few years of visits and letters.

Both comedy and tragedy are found in the story of the Corinthian church. There was the comedy of a dynamic, gifted Christian community composed of uneducated, uninfluential people. They were plucked out of one of the greatest centers of trade, political authority and pagan religion in the Roman Empire. Morals were so bad in Corinth that its citizens had inspired a word for sexual license—to *Corinthianize!* The existence of a church in such a setting was a reason for comic rejoicing.

However, there was also the tragedy of the Corinthians forgetting their humble roots and placing themselves as kings over one another—even over Paul, their founder and friend. The resulting tensions and schisms would boil over with even greater heartache for Paul by the time he was writing 2 Corinthians.

In the first six chapters of 1 Corinthians Paul begins with the distressing matters he has learned about: factions, incest, court cases and freedom gone wild. In chapters 7-14 he treats a series of topics that the Corinthians have asked him about, from marriage to spiritual gifts, with each new topic signaled by the phrase "Now concerning. . . . " Finally, he sums up the teaching of the book in chapter 15, which is devoted to a theology of the resurrection or "last things."

Understanding why chapter 15 and parts of chapters 1-4 fit in this book is the key to unlocking 1 Corinthians. As always, Paul is not only interested in correcting practice but also in grounding his instruction in theological principles. In fact, the Corinthians had two root problems: premature spirituality (they thought they had everything heaven could offer) and immature spirituality (they forgot that the heart of the gospel is love, servanthood and the cross). Perhaps our communities, too, need correction in both practice and theology.

For the sake of simplicity and brevity this study guide generally treats 1 Corinthians chapter by chapter. On three occasions we combined two chapters of the book into one study. We will rely on some cross-references and the leader's notes to clarify thematic overlaps from chapter to chapter, while concentrating on the subjects as they arise naturally in the letter.

If the topics seem to appear haphazardly, try to keep in mind the underlying theological issues at stake throughout the letter. And remember that most of our relationships and communities are pretty haphazard affairs themselves!

Suggestions for Individual Study

1. As you begin each study, pray that God will speak to you through his Word.

2. Read the introduction to the study and respond to the personal reflection question or exercise. This is designed to help you focus on God and on the theme of the study.

3. Each study deals with a particular passage—so that you can delve into the author's meaning in that context. Read and reread the passage to be studied. The questions are written using the language of the New International Version, so you may wish to use that version of the Bible. The New Revised Standard Version is also recommended.

4. This is an inductive Bible study, designed to help you discover for yourself what Scripture is saying. The study includes three types of questions. *Observation* questions ask about the basic facts: who, what, when, where and how. *Interpretation* questions delve into the meaning of the passage. *Application* questions help you discover the implications of the text for growing in Christ. These three keys unlock the treasures of Scripture.

Write your answers to the questions in the spaces provided or in a personal journal. Writing can bring clarity and deeper understanding of yourself and of God's Word.

5. It might be good to have a Bible dictionary handy. Use it to look up any unfamiliar words, names or places.

6. Use the prayer suggestion to guide you in thanking God for what you have learned and to pray about the applications that have come to mind.

7. You may want to go on to the suggestion under "Now or Later," or you may want to use that idea for your next study.

Suggestions for Members of a Group Study

1. Come to the study prepared. Follow the suggestions for individual study mentioned above. You will find that careful preparation will greatly enrich your time spent in group discussion.

2. Be willing to participate in the discussion. The leader of your group will not be lecturing. Instead, he or she will be encouraging the members of the group to discuss what they have learned. The leader will be asking the questions that are found in this guide.

3. Stick to the topic being discussed. Your answers should be based on the verses which are the focus of the discussion and not on outside authorities such as commentaries or speakers. These studies focus on a particular passage of Scripture. Only rarely should you refer to other portions of the Bible. This allows for everyone to participate in in-depth study on equal ground.

4. Be sensitive to the other members of the group. Listen attentively when they describe what they have learned. You may be surprised by their insights! Each question assumes a variety of answers. Many questions do not have "right" answers, particularly questions that aim at meaning or application. Instead the questions push us to explore the passage more thoroughly.

When possible, link what you say to the comments of others. Also, be affirming whenever you can. This will encourage some of the more hesitant members of the group to participate.

5. Be careful not to dominate the discussion. We are sometimes so eager to express our thoughts that we leave too little opportunity for others to respond. By all means participate! But allow others to also.

6. Expect God to teach you through the passage being discussed and through the other members of the group. Pray that you will have an enjoyable and profitable time together, but also that as a result of the study you will find ways that you can take action individually and/or as a group.

7. Remember that anything said in the group is considered confidential and should not be discussed outside the group unless specific permission is given to do so.

8. If you are the group leader, you will find additional suggestions at the back of the guide.

1

Called in Christ

Thankful Together or Falling Apart

1 Corinthians 1

Have you ever found a Christian group that doesn't have any problems? If so, don't join it—you'll ruin everything!

GROUP DISCUSSION. Write down a one-line definition of leadership. Share your definition with the group. One simple but powerful definition of a leader is "someone who others follow." Create a chart with two columns, one listing the pros and the other the cons of following another person. Talk about each member's chart as a whole group. Identify one major leader-follower pitfall you want to avoid as a group.

PERSONAL REFLECTION. Recall a clique in school that you were part of or excluded from. How did your experience with that clique feel?

The church in Corinth was far from perfect. Paul had heard a long list of complaints about this eager but misguided flock. As he attempted some long distance pastoring, where would he begin? Most issues in Christian communities either lead to or are occasioned by divisions. Paul's starting point of conflicts and splits is very relevant for problem groups and individuals today. In this study we will begin to see the spiritual roots of united and divided communities. *Read 1 Corinthians 1:1-9.*

1. Before discussing the problems in Corinth Paul affirms his readers. What does he say about why he is thankful for them?

2. Consider a Christian group that you are part of right now. What is one characteristic of that group that you are grateful for?

How does expressing gratitude to God contribute toward unity in a Christian group?

3. *Read 1 Corinthians 1:10-17.* Why do you think cliques had formed around Paul, Apollos and Cephas (v. 12)?

What do you think the "Christ" party represents (assuming, as is likely, that it is not something positive)?

4. How did Paul conduct himself in Corinth to avoid, if possible, the problem of a personality cult (vv. 14-17)?

5. What evidence of hero worship do you observe in the church today?

What is the main antidote to personality cults and the disunity that they create (v. 13)?

6. *Read 1 Corinthians 1:18-31.* The Corinthians boasted in worldly wisdom and those who taught it. How does the message of the cross destroy all such boasting (vv. 18-25)?

7. The Corinthians also felt intellectually and spiritually superior to others. What had they forgotten about their past and the reason God chose them (vv. 26-29)?

8. How do verses 30-31 sum up the main teaching of this chapter?

9. As you reflect on your past, what reasons do you have for being humble rather than proud?

---

10. How can genuine humility promote unity in your church or fellowship?

Take time to "boast in the Lord," thanking him for all he has done for you.

Now or Later

The theologically full language in 1 Corinthians 1:18-25 could take a lifetime to unpack and apply! Reflect on how you tend to solve problems in your life, and compare how the world attempts to overcome its obstacles. Consider higher education, technology, politics and business. How does a crucified Christ challenge each of these societal structures?

How does the cross shape your everyday decisions?

2

Mind of Christ

True Wisdom from the Spirit

Many people think Christianity is for the mindless and dull. Someone has said, "I feel like unscrewing my head and putting it underneath the pew every time I go to church." Unfortunately, this chapter has been used to support an uneducated, unthinking approach to Christianity. But this misses Paul's point. As Søren Kierkegaard, the Danish philosopher, once said, "Christ doesn't destroy reason; he *dethrones* it." One might add that a maturing Christian, rather than dumbing down, actually becomes wiser in the ways of the Spirit.

GROUP DISCUSSION. Imagine you encounter a confusing Bible passage or really obscure study guide question (hopefully not in this guide!). Brainstorm a list of three or more group responses to such a situation that would not fully reflect that true wisdom comes from God. Contrast this with a list of approaches that do demonstrate our dependence on God's Spirit. You may want to think about actual past group encounters with the Bible that have been or have not been helpful.

PERSONAL REFLECTION. How has Christianity challenged you to think differently?

As we work through this passage, we will discover the true source of wisdom that allows us to grow up in Christ. *Read 1 Corinthians 2:1-5.*

---

1. Greek philosophers were often polished orators whose eloquence and wisdom dazzled their audiences. How does this contrast with Paul's preaching in Corinth?

Why didn't Paul rely on his great wisdom and his obvious communication skills?

---

2. How have Christians today sometimes adopted the world's methods in spreading the gospel?

---

3. *Read 1 Corinthians 2:6-16.* How is God's wisdom different from the wisdom of this age (vv. 6-9)?

Why are *secret* and *hidden* (v. 7) good words to describe this wisdom?

---

4. If God's wisdom is secret and hidden, how can we come to know it and express it (vv. 10-13)?

5. When in your life has God given you understanding or communication ability that went beyond your own natural capacity?

How could these experiences become more frequent in your life?

6. When it comes to understanding God's wisdom, how does the person without the Spirit contrast with the spiritual person (vv. 14-16)?

7. If non-Christians cannot understand the things of the Spirit, how can we talk with them about Christ?

8. *Read 1 Corinthians 3:1-4.* Even though the Corinthians had the Spirit, why couldn't they be considered spiritual?

9. Which category best describes you: a person without the Spirit (2:14), an infant in Christ who is still worldly (3:1) or a spiritual Christian (2:15)? Explain.

10. What can you do to become more spiritually mature (2:6)?

Pray to be filled with the Spirit and to deepen in the wisdom of the Spirit in a fresh way today.

Now or Later

Based on this passage (2:1—3:4), how would you define spiritual maturity?

Identify six or more characteristics of the spiritually mature person. Which characteristic do you most need to see increase in your life?

What difference would such growth make in your everyday experience?

3

Founded on Christ

Working Together with God

1 Corinthians 3:5-23

The Duke of Windsor, recalling his childhood discipline by George V, then king of England, said that his father used to daily remind him, "Never forget who you are." As the spiritual father of the Corinthians Paul reminds them in this chapter, "Never forget *whose* you are."

GROUP DISCUSSION. Create a chart with the following leadership characteristics in column A: (a) persuasive, (b) prayerful, (c) pastoral, (d) perceptive, and (e) passionate. In column B "score" from 1 to 5, 5 being high, how important each characteristic is to the life of a Christian group. Now add up in column C the total score given to each characteristic by the whole group; for example, if "persuasive" was rated 2, 4, 5, 3, 1 and 2 by the members of your group, its total group score would be the sum of the numbers: 17. Which characteristic "won," that is, had the highest group score? Which was lowest? Now take a few minutes to share as a group. Do you agree or disagree with the group results? Why? Did you like this exercise? If your personal pick for top leadership characteristic ended up with a low group rating, how does this feel?

PERSONAL REFLECTION. Upon your death what contribution in life would you most like to be remembered for?

The Corinthians were worldly and quarrelsome because they misunderstood both the message and the messengers of the cross. In chapters one and two, Paul focused on the message—the true wisdom from God. Now he looks at God's messengers. As he does so, Paul reminds the Corinthians and us of our true identity in Christ and how this should shape all Christian ministry. This study will lead to a proper perspective on the place of our ministry in the overall work of God. *Read 1 Corinthians 3:5-23.*

1. What two illustrations does Paul use to describe himself and Apollos (vv. 6-9, 10-15)?

What does Paul compare the church to in each of these illustrations (see also vv. 16-17)?

2. In what ways is God's church like a field being planted (vv. 6-9)?

Why is it foolish to exalt those who work in the field?

3. What task have you been assigned (v. 5) in the garden of God's church?

4. In 3:10-15 Paul changes the metaphor from farming to building. Describe the various ways the church is like a building under construction.

5. What does it mean to be careful how one builds (vv. 10-11)?

How do you feel about the quality of our work being revealed on the day of judgment?

6. In 3:3 Paul accused the Corinthians of being worldly. How can he say to the same people, "You are God's temple" and "God's Spirit lives in you" (v. 16)?

7. What kind of destruction of the temple is Paul thinking about in verse 17?

How do you see Christian communities being destroyed this way today?

8. How does God's passion for his church help us to understand the divine evaluation of ministry that we looked at in question 5?

---

9. The Corinthians had initially claimed "I belong to Paul" or "I belong to Apollos" (1:12 RSV). Paul claims something more important. In what sense do Paul, Apollos and everything else belong to the Corinthians—and to us (vv. 21-23)?

Why should this put an end to "boasting about men" (v. 21)?

---

10. How does this chapter affect your view of your own ministry in the church and that of professional ministers?

Pray that in your ministry you will build with enduring materials on the foundation of Christ. Pray also for those who serve you as leaders.

Now or Later

How does the idea of evaluating our lives apply not only to so-called Christian work but also to other aspects of our vocation in Christ: relationships, family life, occupations, avocations, community involvement and so on?

Which sphere most needs maturing in your life at this time?

4

Servants of Christ

At the End of the Parade

1 Corinthians 4

In the last study Paul called the Corinthians not to forget that they were God's holy temple. Now he calls them and all Christian communities to experience the power of radical servanthood for Christ's sake. St. Francis of Assisi exhibited this when he walked through Muslim battle lines during the Crusades in order to preach to the Sultan. Mother Teresa also was a "fool for Christ" when she bent down to care for a dying beggar in Calcutta. There is power in such actions, even though the wise ones of this age openly shake their heads in disbelief or wag their tongues in scorn or, with modern subtlety, manipulate challenging role models into anemic media symbols or clever marketing tools.

GROUP DISCUSSION. As the year 2000 began, *Time* magazine placed Einstein on the front cover as the Person of the Century and Gandhi on the back cover in an advertisement for a computer company. What does this say about worldly values? How do Christians need to be different?

PERSONAL REFLECTION. How do you feel when you hear about people like St. Francis who give away all they have to the poor or who live sacrificially, like Mother Teresa?

In this study we will see what Paul is calling us to when he says, "imitate me" (4:16). *Read 1 Corinthians 4:1-7.*

---

1. In contrast to the hero worship in Corinth, how do Paul and his coworkers wish to be regarded (vv. 1-2)?

---

2. Above all else, why do you think God requires faithfulness from his servants (v. 2)?

---

3. What standards do we often use to evaluate God's servant-leaders today?

Why does Paul care very little about such judgments (vv. 3-5)?

---

4. How could Paul's perspective be abused by an arrogant leader?

---

5. How has it been dangerous for you in the past to be too tied to human judgments?

On the other hand what are the dangers of being too independent of the counsel of other believers?

---

6. Paul fears the Corinthians are moving "beyond what was written"—probably a reference to the Old Testament Scriptures. How might going beyond the authority of Scripture (and the authority of the God of the Bible) result in taking "pride in one man over against another" (v. 6)?

---

7. What does the proud person fail to realize (v. 7)?

---

8. *Read 1 Corinthians 4:8-17.* Scripture teaches that the suffering of this present age precedes the glory of the age to come. In their own minds, how had the Corinthians taken a shortcut to glory (vv. 8, 10)?

---

9. How did their "glorious" description of themselves contrast with the experiences of Paul and the other apostles (vv. 9-13)?

---

10. Why would the Corinthians and the world look down on the apostles "at the end of the parade" rather than viewing them as great?

11. If you were one of the Corinthians, how would Paul's words make you feel about your attitudes?

12. How would imitating Paul's way of life (vv. 16-17) require changes in your own thinking and actions?

In what ways does this passage challenge you to become a "fool for Christ"?

Pray that God's searchlight would be trained on your deepest attitudes and everyday behavior, and that his Spirit would increasingly conform you to Christ's (and Paul's) example.

Now or Later

Read 1 Corinthians 4:18-21. We receive the first hint in this section that some people in Corinth were not only boasting about other leaders but were also putting down Paul. How does the apostle choose to combat these opponents? Paul is no stranger to miraculous acts and miraculous speech (in other words, obvious, outward expressions of power). But in reviewing all of chapters 1-4, what kind of "kingdom of God" power do you think Paul hopes to observe, and to express in return, when he arrives in Corinth (v. 21)?

5

Members of Christ

The Body Is Meant for the Lord

1 Corinthians 5—6

The ideal of the New Testament church has inspired both exciting and disastrous experiments down through history. Hoping to create the perfect New Testament community, some have tried to design groups where all the gifts are expressed, worship is spontaneous and fellowship is deep. But they forget the common element of all churches—people, who bring problems!

GROUP DISCUSSION. Consider this idea: beliefs lead to behavior. Why did Paul just spend the first quarter of his letter on (mostly) theological matters?

PERSONAL REFLECTION. How do you react when you hear about serious moral and spiritual problems among people in your church?

In chapters 1-4 Paul dealt with division in the church, using that issue as an occasion to establish a lot of spiritual theology. Now he focuses on serious moral problems in Corinth. Incest and drunkenness during communion are hardly what we hope or expect to find in church. But we must remember that growing churches are not always filled with well-scrubbed saints, but rather with a motley collection of sinners being saved. This study presents the basis for purity in the whole church, which must include the lives being led by each individual member. *Read 1 Corinthians 5:1-8.*

---

1. From these verses describe what the society and the church were like.

---

2. How is Paul's strategy of discipline designed to bring health to both the church and the individual (vv. 2-5)?

---

3. Why do you think so few churches today practice this kind of discipline?

How would you feel if you were the recipient of such discipline by the leaders of your church?

---

4. *Read 1 Corinthians 5:9-13.* Some Christians practice a doctrine of "double separation." First, they separate themselves from the evil influences in the world. Second, they separate themselves from Christians who have not separated themselves from the world. What type of separation is taught in these verses (v. 12)?

5. Why is tolerating and associating with immoral people in the church more dangerous than keeping company with immoral people in secular society?

6. *Read 1 Corinthians 6:1-11.* What commands and guidelines does Paul give for settling disputes between Christians (6:1-8)? Explain.

7. Apart from apparently being another current problem in Corinth that calls for a response by Paul, how does this topic fit with the previous section on sexual immorality?

8. In 6:9-10 Paul mentions the kinds of people who will not inherit the kingdom of God. Why do you think he warns us against being deceived about this (6:9)?

9. How and why had the Corinthians changed since becoming Christians (6:11)?

10. *Read 1 Corinthians 6:12-20.* "Everything is permissible for me"

(6:12) was probably a quote from some Corinthians who felt that they were above moral rules and that their bodies had nothing to do with their spiritual lives. What arguments does Paul use to refute this idea?

11. Paul calls the body "a temple of the Holy Spirit" (6:18-20). How does the biblical view of the body presented here contrast with our modern view?

12. How can understanding your body as a temple of the Holy Spirit (6:19) lead you to a healthy balance of bodily control and bodily celebration?

Praise God for the changes that have happened in your life since you met Christ. Ask him to help you take whatever steps are necessary to maintain both personal and corporate purity. Pray for leaders who are facing the challenge of exercising discipline within your community.

Now or Later

13. Paul compares the Christian life to the Passover and the Feast of Unleavened Bread (see Exodus 12). According to Paul, what do yeast, bread without yeast, and the Passover lamb each symbolize (5:6-8)?

14. How does this analogy help us relate to people who bring their pre-Christian lifestyles into the church?

15. How can we distinguish between the kinds of people who should be put out of the church (5:2, 9-11; 6:9-10) and those who belong in the church even though they are still "worldly" and immature (see 3:1)?

16. When is a whip required (4:21), as opposed to a gentle, loving approach?

17. Imagine you are writing a manual about discipline for your church's leadership. What would the main principles and procedures be?

6

Devoted to Christ

Marrying When Time Is Short

What topic do you think you'd find toughest to tackle in preaching?

When a college chaplain asked a student what he'd like to hear a sermon on in the coming year, he got the response, "Homosexuality." Issues surrounding sexuality are tough to tackle, but they are central to our identity as human beings.

GROUP DISCUSSION. If your Christian community has a published position paper on marriage and sexuality, arrange to get copies for the group and read it. What issues are well-handled? Are Scriptures used in support of conclusions? What issues are not covered deeply enough? What does not work for you in the paper? (In the event no such paper exists, you could begin outlining a table of contents for one. If appropriate, you might submit the ideas to your church leaders.)

PERSONAL REFLECTION. If you wrote a letter to Paul today about marriage, sexuality and singleness, what would your main questions be?

Corinth, unlike most modern cities today, did not have sex shops, *Playboy* magazines, porn videos and "adult entertainment" centers. But still there was so much sexual immorality that the ancients had a word to describe engaging in raw sensual pleasure—to *Corinthianize*. In chapter six Paul dealt with those who justified a permissive lifestyle in the name of Christian freedom. In this chapter he battles on the opposite front. Some Corinthians claimed sex was sinful—or at least a second-class diversion—even in marriage. Up to now in the letter, Paul has been reflecting on church problems he has heard about "through the grapevine." But now the big topic of marriage and singleness becomes the first one that he writes about in response to a direct inquiry from the church in Corinth (7:1). Other topics will follow in the letter (introduced by "Now concerning . . . " NASB), but this one is thorny enough to occupy a long chapter all by itself. Working through this passage will allow us to base our view and practice of intimate human relationships on the Scriptures rather than on sentimentality or human philosophy. We will see that the Bible is beautifully practical. *Read 1 Corinthians 7:1-9.*

---

1. Paul begins where he left off in chapter six, with sexual immorality. Although Paul agrees that celibacy is good (v. 1), why is it impractical for most people (vv. 2, 7, 9)?

---

2. What practical advice does Paul give to the unmarried and the married for avoiding sexual immorality (vv. 2-9)?

---

3. Paul's emphasis is not on what a spouse should expect but what a spouse should give (vv. 3-5). Why is this emphasis important?

How would this attitude of giving transform marriages you know (including your own or the one you anticipate)?

4. *Read 7:10-16,* where Paul answers questions about marriage and divorce. How do his statements "to the married" (vv. 10-11) affirm what Jesus had already taught (see Mark 10:2-12)?

---

5. In verses 12-16 Paul discusses a situation not covered by Jesus' teaching in the Gospels—marriages between Christians and non-Christians. Why might a Christian be tempted to divorce a non-Christian?

According to Paul, what are some benefits of remaining in a spiritually mixed marriage? Explain.

---

6. Under what circumstances would Paul seemingly allow for divorce, and why (vv. 15-16)?

Why is Paul's instruction here not an "easy way out?"

---

7. What principles from the chapter so far could help us care for Christians who are considering separation or divorce?

---

8. *Read 1 Corinthians 7:25-40,* where Paul addresses those considering marriage. Why does Paul call singleness a "better" way (v. 38) and a "happier" way (v. 40) when he has such a high view of marriage?

9. Taking the chapter as a whole, what considerations would help a couple decide whether to marry, to wait or to separate?

Which of these considerations apply to your life or the lives of those you are close to right now?

Ask God to help you be faithful and devoted to him in your relationships, your job and the other areas of your life. Pray for your own marriage, present or future, that it would reflect the principles of this passage. Pray also for married or divorced people in your circle. Finally, pray that any unbelieving spouses would be brought to Christ.

Now or Later

10. *Read 1 Corinthians 7:17-24,* where Paul counsels those who think they are in the wrong situation in life. How does Paul explain and illustrate the "rule" that applies to such people?

11. Paul speaks of God calling us to a certain situation (vv. 17, 24) and of God calling us while we were in that situation (vv. 18-22). How are these two dimensions of calling different?

12. What difference should being called by God make if we are in a difficult marriage or an unsatisfying job?

7

Living for Christ

The Right to Relinquish Rights

1 Corinthians 8—9

A note tacked up on a refrigerator had these words: "It is better to be righteous than right!" Today individuals and groups are clamoring and clashing over rights: the right to free speech, the rights of the poor, the right to liberation, women's rights, aboriginal rights, the right to not be bothered by smokers (or nonsmokers), the rights of animals, the rights of blacks, the rights of adoptees . . .

GROUP DISCUSSION. Look at the list in the introduction above. Brainstorm at least ten more groups fighting for rights today. You may even make up a couple of new ones! Which of these groups has the most legitimate claims and causes? Evangelical Christians in North America are often marginalized in the media and society as a whole. Should they lobby for better treatment? Why or why not? How would trying to protect persecuted Christians in other countries be a different matter?

PERSONAL REFLECTION. How do you react when you know you are right and yet someone continues openly to oppose you?

So many of the struggles over rights, both those very legitimate and those less so, seem to revolve around attaining freedom to change the status quo. The apostle Paul, however, appears to be on opposite ground. He has just written about remaining in the situation God calls us to, whether that is slavery or singleness, and remaining in step with God's commands (7:17-24). Now we will see that Paul indeed practices what he preaches. For him, rights and freedoms are unimportant compared to the privilege of living for Christ. This study aims to move us away from running for ourselves and toward running for Christ. *Read 1 Corinthians 8:1-13.*

---

1. Sacrificial animals offered in temples were dedicated to a pagan god, and most of them were sold in the public market. Understandably, many Christians in Corinth wondered whether they should eat such meat. According to Paul, what do mature Christians know about food sacrificed to idols (vv. 4-6, 8)?

What warning does Paul give about this kind of knowledge (vv. 1-3)? Explain.

---

2. What does Paul say is more important than exercising the freedom that comes from knowledge (vv. 9-13)?

---

3. What "knowledge" and freedom that you currently enjoy would you be willing to give up in order to not destroy a weaker brother?

4. How can the behavior of a mature believer challenge an immature believer to grow?

5. Read 1 Corinthians 9:1-18. Paul moves on from rights and freedoms based on knowledge to the topic of rights based on position. What apostolic rights has Paul given up (9:4-5, 11-12, 14, 18)?

6. How can receiving financial benefits, even a mere living, as a preacher sometimes hinder the gospel (9:12)?

7. What practical choices have you made in your life that might be hindering the spread of the gospel?

8. Read 1 Corinthians 9:19-27. How and why has Paul given up the freedom to live whatever lifestyle he prefers (9:19-23)?

9. How might we adjust our lifestyles in order to reach people in various subcultures?

How might being sensitive to a particular group's struggles for justice be part of this?

What is God leading you to do in this in response to this?

10. Can we go too far in the "contextualizing" of the gospel? Explain. (For example, how about taking on the religious practices of Islam for the sake of Muslim evangelization?)

11. In giving up the rights mentioned in chapters 8-9, how are we like athletes in training (9:24-27)?

Ask God to help you train more rigorously for the "game" of relinquishing rights for the sake of love and the gospel, so you will not be disqualified but will receive the victor's crown.

Now or Later

12. Paul says that he cannot boast about preaching the gospel, because that is required of him (9:16-17). But he can "boast" (v. 15) if he does something beyond what is required, namely, to preach free of charge. This is what he has voluntarily chosen to do, and he will be rewarded accordingly. In what ways might we go beyond the call of duty as Christians in order to receive a heavenly reward?

13. How could you shape your life in order to receive enough from your paying job to live on and have creative time for intentional, free-of-charge gospel ministry as well? Or how could you use your career to enter and incarnate the gospel in a restricted-access country?

8

Eating with Christ

All for the Glory of God

1 Corinthians 10

Should Christians go to R-rated movies—or any movies for that matter? Should they drink alcoholic beverages such as beer or wine? Should they wear expensive clothes, makeup and jewelry? Debates over such "questionable" practices are as old as the church. How can we resolve them?

GROUP DISCUSSION. Consider if you became the subject of a book in the Bible. If a chronicler wrote the history of your study group (or church), what are the choices, events and programs you would be most proud of? On the other hand, which (questionable) episodes would you hope he would leave out of the account? Explain.

PERSONAL REFLECTION. What "questionable" practices have you wrestled with personally?

The Corinthians were divided over such issues. Some had overscrupulous consciences. They would not sit down to a meal if the meat had been purchased at a pagan meat market (and therefore offered to a "god"). Others were so "liberated" that they could participate in the

Lord's Supper or Communion and then commit acts of sexual immorality. These liberated Christians regarded baptism and Communion as automatic protection against God's judgment. In 1 Corinthians 10 Paul finds a way of reaching both kinds of people: he calls them and us to do everything for the glory of God. In this study we return to the idea that every behavior is not beneficial, and thus seek to bring appropriate discipline into our lives. *Read 1 Corinthians 10:1-13.*

---

1. What experiences did all the Israelites have in common when they left Egypt and headed for the Promised Land?

Why was God not pleased with them?

---

2. Why does Paul remind the Corinthians (and us) of these events?

---

3. Reflect on a time when you forgot the Lord's goodness and fell into grumbling. How did you become aware that you were testing the Lord's patience?

---

4. How does Paul counter the idea that some temptations are just too strong to be resisted?

5. Think of one or two areas where you are currently experiencing temptation. In which one of these are you least likely to believe that there is a way of escape?

In what way has God in fact provided an escape in the midst of your temptation?

6. *Read 1 Corinthians 10:14-22.* Why are some lifestyles incompatible with celebrating Communion (the Lord's Supper or the Eucharist)?

7. Although Paul is dealing with a pastoral problem rather than doctrine, what does he teach us about the sacredness of the Lord's Supper?

Describe your attitude in approaching Communion and worship in general.

8. *Read 1 Corinthians 10:23-33.* According to these verses, what principles should guide our behavior as Christians?

9. What practices in your life do you consider "permissible" but possibly not beneficial or constructive (v. 23)?

How can the principles discussed in this passage guide your behavior in these specific areas?

Pray that God would deepen in your heart and life this double truth, as taught by Martin Luther: "The Christian is a most free lord of all, subject to none. The Christian is a most submissive servant, subject to all."

Now or Later

How does Paul apply the principles of 10:23-33 to the subject of eating meat offered to idols? Paul clearly exhibits a strong emphasis on the voluntary limitation of personal freedom for the good of others and the gospel. Why then does he still suggest that he is ultimately free from judgment no matter what his behavior in regard to disputable matters like idol meat (see the apparent aside in 10:29-30)? How is following the Spirit for the sake of the gospel different than following a rule?

9

Headship of Christ
Truly Worshiping Together

1 Corinthians 11

Two trends in Western society contrive to make us independent people: the trend to blur the differences between the sexes (androgyny) and the human potential movement. In the movie *Tootsie* a male actor impersonating a woman said to a woman with whom he fell in love, "I was a better man with you when I was a woman than I am a woman with you now that I am a man." Such is the sexual confusion produced by the first trend. Fritz Perls verbalized the second trend this way: "I do my thing and you do your thing and if by chance we meet, it's beautiful."

GROUP DISCUSSION. On a scale of 1 to 10, with 10 being most positive, how would you rate your group experience in the following categories: (1) reverence toward God, (2) respect for one another, (3) relationship between men and women, (4) preparation for worship, (5) practical service to one another. What category needs most improvement? How do all the categories fit together?

PERSONAL REFLECTION. When you enter a worship service, do you tend to think mainly of your personal relationship with God or your relationship with your fellow worshipers?

Both trends mentioned above work against our newness in Christ. Followers of Jesus are neither independent nor dependent but interdependent. In 1 Cor-inthians 10 (study 8) we explored our interdependence in matters of conscience, though the theme of worship and body life was also introduced (10:17). Now we more fully discover our interdependence in Christian worship and fellowship. This passage will challenge us to see worship as both a "vertical" honoring of God and a "horizontal" honoring of one another. *Read 1 Corinthians 11:1-16.*

---

1. What seems to be Paul's major concern for the church in this section?

---

2. The word *head* in verse 3 could either mean "chief" and "ruler" or "source" and "origin" (like the head of a stream). Which understanding of headship best fits Paul's concern here? Explain.

---

3. In light of the headship described in verse 3, why was it wrong for a man to pray or prophesy with his head covered (vv. 4-10)?

Whether you are a man or a woman, how is it possible to forget who

God is and who you are when you enter into worship?

---

4. In the culture of Corinth a woman signaled that she was in right relationship with her husband either by wearing a veil that covered her hair or by wearing her hair up (rather than letting it fall loose). What reasons does Paul give for continuing this practice (vv. 4-10, 13-16)?

---

5. Paul balances his previous statements by saying that "in the Lord" man is not independent of woman (vv. 11-12). Why is this balance important?

What difference will this truth make in your relationship to the opposite sex?

---

6. Although we may not have a cultural equivalent for head coverings and have to admit (illustrated by the NIV footnote on vv. 4-7) that the precise practice in Corinth remains obscure anyway, how

should appropriate relationships between men and women be
expressed in Christian community?

---

7. *Read 1 Corinthians 11:17-34.* In New Testament times Communion
was celebrated during a common meal or "love feast." What abuses
had crept into this celebration (vv. 18-22)?

---

8. What is the purpose and significance of the Lord's Supper (vv. 23-
27)?

In the light of this, why would eating and drinking "without recognizing the body of the Lord" be so dangerous (vv. 29-32)?

---

9. According to Paul, how can we eat and drink the Lord's Supper in a
worthy manner (v. 28-34)?

How will you prepare yourself to participate on the next occasion the
Lord's Supper is celebrated in your community?

10. What has this chapter taught you overall about worship that is honoring or dishonoring to God?

Where there has been pain in your relationship with the opposite sex and where this has intruded on worship, ask God for forgiveness and healing. Where other resentments and conflict are disrupting the celebration of the Lord's Supper in your church, pray for the power of love and unity to break through.

Now or Later

11. Head coverings also symbolized the differences between the sexes. According to Paul, what differences between men and women have been built into creation by God himself (vv. 7-10)?

12. How can one understand the language of verse 7 in a manner that does not marginalize a woman's position in relationship to God?

13. Why is it important, even in the face of current cultural pressures, to maintain a biblical distinctiveness for each gender?

10

Body of Christ

Manifestations for the Common Good

1 Corinthians 12

Imagine designing a church in which most members sit passively, where one or two gifts are exalted, and others are made to feel dispensable. Sound familiar?

The church today has enormous frozen assets. Only when we thaw these assets and release every member for ministry can the work of God be done in the world. After several decades of teaching on "gifts," we have made surprisingly little progress. One reason is that gifts have been co-opted by the human potential movement. We view our gifts as part of our development and fulfillment rather than as one more glorious way to be interdependent in Christ.

GROUP DISCUSSION. Every personal strength seems to have a shadow side that is negative. Create a chart with column A being the following classic roles in group life: (a) leadership, (b) teaching, (c) spiritual insight, (d) administering projects, (e) extending mercy to people, (f) evangelism, (g) prayer. You can add one or two more that occur to you. In column B jot down one line as to how each gift could contribute to a Christian group. In column C describe briefly how each gift, improperly expressed, could hurt a group. Finally, choose (and share) the one gift that seems to be most often the role that you play in the study group.

PERSONAL REFLECTION. How do you respond when you are told that you have a gift or talent vitally needed by the group to which you belong?

In this study we will examine the source and significance of spiritual gifts. *Read 1 Corinthians 12.*

1. What words, phrases and themes do you see repeated through the passage?

2. What particular problem in the Corinthian church may have led Paul to offer the "test" in verse 3?

3. What do verses 4-6 reveal about the unity and diversity of spiritual gifts?

4. Paul calls each gift a "manifestation of the Spirit" (v. 7). In what ways does the Spirit manifest himself in the church, and why (vv. 7-11)?

5. Compare the gift inventory with that provided in the group discussion above. How would experiencing the full range of gifts in verses 8-10 change the life of your group?

What new roles might you be drawn to play in your community?

---

6. What might make some members of your church feel useless or envious of other parts of the body?

Has this ever been true for you? Explain.

---

7. How does Paul respond to the problem of feeling dispensable (vv. 14-20)?

---

8. What might make some members of your church feel self-sufficient or superior (v. 21)?

---

9. According to Paul, how can we make every part of the body feel special (vv. 21-26)?

How could you apply these principles in your church or group?

---

10. Paul does not give us a complete list of gifts in this chapter. What might the words *first, second, third* and *then* (v. 28) indicate?

11. What can you do to help others in your group or church to discover their giftedness?

What do you think will happen to your own gifts when you do this?

Ask for spiritual gifts to be released or recognized in your group, in your church and in you. Pray that all these gifts would operate in unity, for the common good.

Now or Later

12. How do you reconcile Paul's exhortation to "eagerly desire the greater gifts" (v. 31) with his earlier emphasis that God sovereignly assigns gifts (vv. 11, 18, 28)?

_____

13. Do you think this is an exhortation for each individual, something for the whole Christian community to hear and consider, or both?

_____

14. How is 12:7 summed up in the following quotation: "Sir, you wish to serve God and go to heaven. Then you must find companions or make them, for the Bible knows nothing of solitary religion" (advice given to John Wesley)?

11

Love of Christ

The Most Excellent Way

1 Corinthians 13

Perhaps the most abused phrase in the English language is "I love you." Instead of communicating unselfish caring, it often expresses enlightened self-interest, manipulative affection or sheer lust.

GROUP DISCUSSION. Take time for each member to write out a definition of love. Compare your definitions. Keep these ideas in mind as you look at Paul's approach to the topic. Where do you see such love operating in your group? in your church?

PERSONAL REFLECTION. Think of a person who has truly loved you. What were the marks of that person's way of relating to you?

In 1 Corinthians 13 Paul not only defines love for us but shows us why this is the most excellent way to relate to anyone—especially to members of the family of God. The biblical view of love provides a context for gift ministry and all body life. *Read 1 Corinthians 13.*

1. This chapter has been called "a pure and perfect gem, perhaps the noblest assemblage of beautiful thoughts in beautiful language extant in our world" (H. Alford). What are your main impressions after reading the chapter as a whole?

2. What is so tragic about using our gifts without love (vv. 1-3)?

How can we know whether our personal ministry is marked by such lovelessness?

3. How would you define each of love's qualities (vv. 4-7)?

Which aspect of love do you most need to develop?

4. In verses 8-13 Paul summarizes the supremacy of love. Compared with love, why do the gifts have limited value?

5. Some understand the "perfection" in verse 10 as the completed New Testament, thus eliminating the need for tongues or prophecy today. Others understand it as the perfection we will experience when Christ returns. In light of Paul's other comparisons (vv. 11-12), which interpretation seems more likely? Explain.

6. How is love greater than faith or hope (v. 13)?

7. Why is love the ultimate solution to the divisions in Corinth or in any church?

8. Considering again the qualities in verses 4-7, how can love lead to healthy interdependence in our relationships rather than unhealthy independence or dependence?

Ask God to infiltrate love into every gift that you express in the body of Christ, reflecting the following truth: "Love is not a gift. . . . It lies at the very heart of all gifts." (A. Bittlinger, Gifts and Graces [Grand Rapids, Mich.: Eerdmans, 1967], p. 75).

Now or Later

In presenting such an absolute description of love, Paul seems to be begging the question of where we get such love. It is widely known that the special Christian word for love, *agape*, means the kind of unconditional, self-sacrificing love shown to us by Jesus. Besides telling us what love is and how gifts should be expressed in love, this passage gives us an incidental portrait of Jesus as the ultimate lover. Reread verses 4-7, replacing *love* with *Jesus*. What fresh picture of Jesus' care do you gain through this exercise?

12

Speaking for Christ

Mature & Orderly Worship

1 Corinthians 14

Words are cheap today. They can be digitized and processed. With one depressed button on a computer we can eliminate words forever. However, the Bible says words have great power because they are an extension of our personality. God's Word, especially, always accomplishes his purposes because it is spoken with his personal power.

GROUP DISCUSSION. Read the general note section in the leader's notes. To get the "cards on the table" have each member identify anything from the list of possible objections to inspired speech which indeed does trouble them. What has been their actual experience? End by reaffirming the commitment to get something positive and fresh out of Paul's teaching, and to maintain a loving stance. (To fail in love at this point would be ironic given the previous chapter!)

PERSONAL REFLECTION. Recall a time when something that was shared from the congregation during a worship service (or in a small group) truly encouraged you. What characterized this word ministry?

In this chapter Paul focuses on the exciting potential of God-inspired speech in the Christian community. Having established in chapter 13 that love should motivate and shape all the gifts, Paul now turns to a concrete example of love ministry through inspired speech. But like every exciting gift, there are abuses to be understood and regulated, as we shall soon see. *Read 1 Corinthians 14:1-25.*

---

1. Evidently, the Corinthians placed great value on the gift of tongues. What do verses 1-5 reveal about why Paul prefers prophecy to (uninterpreted) tongues?

---

2. What illustrations does Paul use to show why (uninterpreted) tongues do not build up the church (vv. 6-12)?

What remedy does Paul suggest (vv. 13-19)?

---

3. In what ways might we be guilty of meaningless or mindless worship today?

How can Paul's counsel improve the quality of your contribution in worship?

4. What does Paul say about the purpose of tongues and of prophecy (vv. 20-25)?

Why would prophetic speech rather than tongues cause visitors to sense God in our midst (vv. 23-25)?

5. *Read 1 Corinthians 14:26-40.* What guidelines does Paul give for when people should speak in tongues and when they should remain silent (vv. 27-28)?

6. Under what circumstances should prophets speak or remain silent, and why (vv. 29-33)?

7. What regulations does Paul give women about speaking or remaining silent, and why (vv. 33-35)?

8. How can Paul's statements here be harmonized with his teaching about women (apparently) routinely praying and prophesying publicly (11:5)?

---

9. Some worship services are so "orderly" that they put us to sleep. Others are so "free" that they seem out of control. How does this chapter promote both freedom and order in our worship?

Which aspect of worship do you feel a need for and why?

Using a paradigm first introduced by Charles Hummel, pray that God would either provide more fire in your public worship or more fireplace (order and structure) to provide a meaningful and safe context for the fire that is somewhat out of control when you meet together.

Now or Later

Reread 1 Corinthains 14:26-40. Based on this passage and Paul's statements about the Lord's Supper in 11:17-34, try to reconstruct a typical worship service in Corinth. A great resource for picturing early Christian worship is Robert Banks's *Going to Church in the First Century,* 2nd ed. (Parramatta, Australia: Hexagon, 1985). What elements would you like to see more of in your community's worship?

13

Hope in Christ

The Resurrection & the Life

1 Corinthians 15—16

Some would say that the most important question, and one always lurking at the edge of our consciousness, is "What happens after death?" Do we live on as disembodied souls, as the Greeks taught? Do we go through countless cycles of reincarnation, as the Hindus believe? Do both body and soul cease to exist, as naturalism maintains?

GROUP DISCUSSION. How did your view of life after death change when you came to Christ or began seeking him? What is the greatest fear about death you still have?

PERSONAL REFLECTION. How do you react when asked to think or talk about life after death?

Because of their Greek heritage, the Corinthians questioned the reality of the resurrection. In this passage Paul challenges their thinking by pointing out the absurd conclusions to which it leads. He reminds us that the resurrection is a crucial aspect of our hope in Christ. *Read 1 Corinthians 15:1-11.*

1. Paul reminds the Corinthians of the gospel he preached to them. What are the essential elements of the gospel?

What importance does the resurrection of Christ play in Paul's gospel?

2. *Read 15:12-34.* If there is no resurrection, what are the consequences for Christ, for Paul and for us (vv. 12-19)?

3. Why is "fallen asleep" (vv. 18, 20) a good way to describe the dead in Christ?

4. How will Christ's resurrection overcome the effects of Adam's sin (vv. 21-28)?

What is one area of your life where you need to experience more victory in Christ?

---

5. How does belief or disbelief in the resurrection affect a person's lifestyle?

How can your lifestyle affect your witness to a world bent on "eating and drinking"?

---

6. *Read 1 Corinthians 15:35-49.* What illustrations does Paul use to explain why the resurrection is not illogical but makes good sense (vv. 35-41)?

---

7. Although the resurrection body is somehow related to the natural body, how is it also radically different (vv. 42-49)?

---

8. What are you most looking forward to in your heavenly existence with Christ?

9. *Read 1 Corinthians 15:50-58.* What message is there in these verses for those who grow weary of this physical world and long to escape to heaven?

10. What is the most substantial change that studying 1 Corinthians has brought about in your life or group?

Ask God to confirm and apply the most vital truths of Corinthians in your heart and life, and to transform your community as a result.

Now or Later

11. *Read 1 Corinthians 16.* What illustrations of "the work of the Lord" (which Paul referred to in 15:58) does this chapter give?

12. To which specific area of service will you give yourself this week, knowing that your labor in the Lord is not in vain?

Leader's Notes

Leading a Bible discussion can be an enjoyable and rewarding experience. But it can also be *scary*—especially if you've never done it before. If this is your feeling, you're in good company. When God asked Moses to lead the Israelites out of Egypt, he replied, "O Lord, please send someone else to do it"! (Ex 4:13). It was the same with Solomon, Jeremiah and Timothy, but God helped these people in spite of their weaknesses, and he will help you as well.

You don't need to be an expert on the Bible or a trained teacher to lead a Bible discussion. The idea behind these inductive studies is that the leader guides group members to discover for themselves what the Bible has to say. This method of learning will allow group members to remember much more of what is said than a lecture would.

These studies are designed to be led easily. As a matter of fact, the flow of questions through the passage from observation to interpretation to application is so natural that you may feel that the studies lead themselves. This study guide is also flexible. You can use it with a variety of groups—student, professional, neighborhood or church groups. Each study takes forty-five to sixty minutes in a group setting.

There are some important facts to know about group dynamics and encouraging discussion. The suggestions listed below should enable you to effectively and enjoyably fulfill your role as leader.

Preparing for the Study

1. Ask God to help you understand and apply the passage in your own life. Unless this happens, you will not be prepared to lead others. Pray too for the various members of the group. Ask God to open your hearts to the message of his Word and motivate you to action.

2. Read the introduction to the entire guide to get an overview of the entire book and the issues which will be explored.

3. As you begin each study, read and reread the assigned Bible passage to familiarize yourself with it.

4. This study guide is based on the New International Version of the Bible.

It will help you and the group if you use this translation as the basis for your study and discussion.

5. Carefully work through each question in the study. Spend time in meditation and reflection as you consider how to respond.

6. Write your thoughts and responses in the space provided in the study guide. This will help you to express your understanding of the passage clearly.

7. It might help to have a Bible dictionary handy. Use it to look up any unfamiliar words, names or places. (For additional help on how to study a passage, see chapter five of *How to Lead a LifeBuilder Study*, IVP, 2018.)

8. Consider how you can apply the Scripture to your life. Remember that the group will follow your lead in responding to the studies. They will not go any deeper than you do.

9. Once you have finished your own study of the passage, familiarize yourself with the leader's notes for the study you are leading. These are designed to help you in several ways. First, they tell you the purpose the study guide author had in mind when writing the study. Take time to think through how the study questions work together to accomplish that purpose. Second, the notes provide you with additional background information or suggestions on group dynamics for various questions. This information can be useful when people have difficulty understanding or answering a question. Third, the leader's notes can alert you to potential problems you may encounter during the study.

10. If you wish to remind yourself of anything mentioned in the leader's notes, make a note to yourself below that question in the study.

Leading the Study

1. Begin the study on time. Open with prayer, asking God to help the group to understand and apply the passage.

2. Be sure that everyone in your group has a study guide. Encourage the group to prepare beforehand for each discussion by reading the introduction to the guide and by working through the questions in the study.

3. At the beginning of your first time together, explain that these studies are meant to be discussions, not lectures. Encourage the members of the group to participate. However, do not put pressure on those who may be hesitant to speak during the first few sessions. You may want to suggest the following guidelines to your group.

☐ Stick to the topic being discussed.

☐ Your responses should be based on the verses which are the focus of the discussion and not on outside authorities such as commentaries or speakers. These studies focus on a particular passage of Scripture. Only rarely should you refer to other portions of the Bible. This allows for everyone to participate in in-depth study on equal ground.

☐ Anything said in the group is considered confidential and will not be discussed outside the group unless specific permission is given to do so.

☐ We will listen attentively to each other and provide time for each person present to talk.

☐ We will pray for each other.

4. Have a group member read the introduction at the beginning of the discussion.

5. Every session begins with a group discussion question. The question or activity is meant to be used before the passage is read. The question introduces the theme of the study and encourages group members to begin to open up. Encourage as many members as possible to participate, and be ready to get the discussion going with your own response.

This section is designed to reveal where our thoughts or feelings need to be transformed by Scripture. That is why it is especially important not to read the passage before the discussion question is asked. The passage will tend to color the honest reactions people would otherwise give because they are, of course, supposed to think the way the Bible does.

You may want to supplement the group discussion question with an icebreaker to help people to get comfortable. See the community section of the *Small Group Starter Kit* (IVP, 1995) for more ideas.

You also might want to use the personal reflection question with your group. Either allow a time of silence for people to respond individually or discuss it together.

6. Have a group member (or members if the passage is long) read aloud the passage to be studied. Then give people several minutes to read the passage again silently so that they can take it all in.

7. Question 1 will generally be an overview question designed to briefly survey the passage. Encourage the group to look at the whole passage, but try to avoid getting sidetracked by questions or issues that will be addressed later in the study.

8. As you ask the questions, keep in mind that they are designed to be used just as they are written. You may simply read them aloud. Or you may prefer to express them in your own words.

There may be times when it is appropriate to deviate from the study guide. For example, a question may have already been answered. If so, move on to the next question. Or someone may raise an important question not covered in the guide. Take time to discuss it, but try to keep the group from going off on tangents.

9. Avoid answering your own questions. If necessary, repeat or rephrase them until they are clearly understood. Or point out something you read in the leader's notes to clarify the context or meaning. An eager group quickly

becomes passive and silent if they think the leader will do most of the talking.
10. Don't be afraid of silence. People may need time to think about the question before formulating their answers.
11. Don't be content with just one answer. Ask, "What do the rest of you think?" or "Anything else?" until several people have given answers to the question.
12. Acknowledge all contributions. Try to be affirming whenever possible. Never reject an answer. If it is clearly off-base, ask, "Which verse led you to that conclusion?" or again, "What do the rest of you think?"
13. Don't expect every answer to be addressed to you, even though this will probably happen at first. As group members become more at ease, they will begin to truly interact with each other. This is one sign of healthy discussion.
14. Don't be afraid of controversy. It can be very stimulating. If you don't resolve an issue completely, don't be frustrated. Move on and keep it in mind for later. A subsequent study may solve the problem.
15. Periodically summarize what the group has said about the passage. This helps to draw together the various ideas mentioned and gives continuity to the study. But don't preach.
16. At the end of the Bible discussion you may want to allow group members a time of quiet to work on an idea under "Now or Later." Then discuss what you experienced. Or you may want to encourage group members to work on these ideas between meetings. Give an opportunity during the session for people to talk about what they are learning.
17. Conclude your time together with conversational prayer, adapting the prayer suggestion at the end of the study to your group. Ask for God's help in following through on the commitments you've made.
18. End on time.
Many more suggestions and helps are found in *How to Lead a LifeBuilder Study*.

Components of Small Groups

A healthy small group should do more than study the Bible. There are four components to consider as you structure your time together.

Nurture. Small groups help us to grow in our knowledge and love of God. Bible study is the key to making this happen and is the foundation of your small group.

Community. Small groups are a great place to develop deep friendships with other Christians. Allow time for informal interaction before and after each study. Plan activities and games that will help you get to know each other. Spend time having fun together—going on a picnic or cooking dinner together.

Worship and prayer. Your study will be enhanced by spending time praising God together in prayer or song. Pray for each other's needs—and keep track of how God is answering prayer in your group. Ask God to help you to apply what you are learning in your study.

Outreach. Reaching out to others can be a practical way of applying what you are learning, and it will keep your group from becoming self-focused. Host a series of evangelistic discussions for your friends or neighbors. Clean up the yard of an elderly friend. Serve at a soup kitchen together, or spend a day working in the community.

Many more suggestions and helps in each of these areas are found in the *Small Group Starter Kit.* You will also find information on building a small group. Reading through the starter kit will be worth your time.

Study 1. 1 Corinthians 1.
Called in Christ.
Purpose: To understand the root causes of and antidotes to divisions within Christian groups and churches.
General note. Paul begins his letter dealing with first things first. What could be more disruptive than quarreling and divisions in the body? But what surprises us is that Paul couches his treatment of the problem in the context of wisdom. You should beware of identifying this wisdom with the positive Old Testament variety found in Proverbs. Paul isn't attacking wisdom from God but rather the worldly wisdom that leads to boasting, quarreling and factions. He wants to introduce the mature to the true way of wisdom, which leads to humility, unity and a weakness that appears foolish to most. This theme will occupy much of the first four chapters of 1 Corinthians.
Group discussion. Make sure some paper and pens are available (actually, this is a good idea for every group discussion). To save time you could skip formulating and sharing definitions of leadership and move right to doing the pro and con chart. The point of this exercise is to explore the damaging foolishness of certain ways of relating to leaders.
Question 1. Paul gives a comprehensive list of the positive facets of the church in Corinth, including (a) it has generally received grace from God in Jesus Christ, including every spiritual gift, specifically the spiritual gifts of knowledge and speaking; (b) the fact that the gospel of the historic Christ (Paul's testimony) is reflected in the community, as well as a desire to see Jesus revealed more fully in history (probably a reference to the anticipated second coming of Christ); (c) the certainty that the church will be kept legally blameless, spiritually vital, and experientially in fellowship with Christ until the end of time. A key insight is to see that these occasions for gratitude all find their source in the faithful character of God (v. 9). If your

group already knows something of the problems in Corinth, you could speculate why Paul is stressing God as the source of gifts ("you have been enriched") at this early point in the letter. Also, speech and knowledge are going to be touchy topics between Paul and the Corinthians. For Paul, true knowledge fundamentally means understanding the good news available in Jesus Christ (E. D. Schmitz, "γινώσκω," *International Dictionary of New Testament Theology,* ed. Colin Brown [Grand Rapids, Mich.: Zondervan, 1976], 2:403). Logos or speech ought to flow from and reflect this knowledge. What is Paul trying to accomplish by mentioning these gifts (v. 5) as belonging to them?

Question 3. Paul was the founder of the church in Corinth and had kept close ties with it. Naturally many would be loyal to their spiritual father who was obviously a gifted leader.

Apollos was a Jew from Alexandria who became a Christian in Ephesus shortly after Paul left Corinth. He was sent to Achaia (the Roman province of which Corinth was a chief city) where "he was a great help to those who by grace had believed" (Acts 18:24-28). It is not surprising that some would want to become his followers.

We are not sure if the reference to the famous apostle Cephas (or Peter—both names mean "rock" but in different languages) indicates a visit by Peter to Corinth or simply the presence of believers influenced by him.

The group that claimed to follow Christ probably refers to the most insidious faction of all. Evidently this group felt and acted spiritually superior to the other groups who followed merely human leaders.

Beyond the historical background it is important to speculate about the spiritual roots of factions in the church. Insight about divisions in Christian communities helps to link the parts of 1 Corinthians 1 together. In short, factions are a reflection of our fallen, prideful human condition. To have the wisdom to choose and support the best leader (vv. 10-17) is to prove, and allow the flaunting of, one's intellectual, social and, ultimately, spiritual superiority (vv. 18-29).

Question 4. Paul does demonstrate wise leadership practice, putting himself at the periphery and Christ at the center. However, practice for Paul always follows belief. The transition to Paul's main theological response to the problems of quarreling and division comes at verse 17. The four key biblical themes introduced in this verse are the gospel, wisdom, the cross of Christ and power. These form the framework for the rest of this chapter and the next three, and play an important role in the whole letter. Don't worry if the group doesn't yet understand these concepts. They will be covered in detail later.

Question 6. Aristides said that on every street in Corinth one met a so-called wise man, who offered his own solutions to the world's problems. The Greeks were intensely interested in philosophic discussions (see Acts 17:21) and often followed their own favorite philosopher. When Paul and his companions came to Corinth, they were viewed within this framework. The Corinthians assumed Paul, Apollos and Cephas were a new kind of wise man and that the gospel was simply a new kind of wisdom. Typically, they aligned themselves with one leader or another and began quarreling over who was the best. Paul attempts to show that they misunderstand both the message and the messengers of the cross, which are considered foolish by the world. Throughout the next three chapters he argues that "the foolishness of God is wiser than man's wisdom, and the weakness of God is stronger than man's strength" (1 Cor 1:25).

Question 7. Pride was the ultimate cause of quarreling and divisions in Corinth. Each group thought its leader was superior, its teaching most profound and its members most distinguished. Paul shatters this notion by reminding them that they were and are the poor, downtrodden nobodies of the world and most often literally drawn from the social margins of the city. That is why God chose them, not because of their imagined superiority. With wonderful "ironic comedy" God makes clear the true outlines of his mercy and power as he works out his plan to make the last first.

Question 8. Encourage the group to explore how Christ has become our wisdom, righteousness, holiness and redemption—as well as our source of pride. Focusing on Jesus offers the best protection against putting leaders on precarious pedestals, and establishes the best foundation for building true unity in our "comm-unity."

Question 10. Help the group take what they have learned about the sources of disunity and turn them around into positive principles of community building: preferring the "foolishness" of God over the "wisdom" of people, remembering our own roots and boasting in the Lord rather than in his messengers.

Study 2. 1 Corinthians 2:1—3:4. Mind of Christ.

Purpose: To learn how we receive and apply the true wisdom we have in Christ so that we grow up in him toward maturity.

General note. Paul tends to use compact, rich language that can seem complex. Don't lose the main threads! In chapter 2 Paul continues to contrast the wisdom of the world and the wisdom of God. This contrast is seen first in the style of Paul's ministry in Corinth (vv. 1-5, 13). His message did not depend on wise words of the world but on powerful words of the cross. Paul then maintains that the world did not recognize the secret wisdom of God, wisdom that has to do with the power of the crucifixion (vv. 6-9, 14). Finally, he insists that it is only by the Spirit that one can receive and understand the wisdom of God (vv. 10-12, 15-16).

You must be careful not to divorce this chapter from the wider issues of 1 Corinthians. Throughout the epistle Paul hints at the tragedy of tasting the things of the Spirit, as the Corinthians certainly had, and yet still missing out on the true wisdom of God. This spiritual gap produced the very sorts of immature belief and behavior that generate the bulk of Paul's concerned response in this letter.

Question 1. We must understand 2:1-5 in its historical and cultural context. Compared to the Greek orators of his day, Paul's speaking didn't measure up ("In person he is unimpressive and his speaking amounts to nothing," 2 Cor 10:10). Yet Paul's sermons demonstrated rhetorical power and a sensitive shaping of his message to fit the audience. Further, in his writing—including this epistle to the Corinthians—Paul frequently employed literary devices that would be very much at home in Greek letters of his day ("His letters are weighty and forceful," 2 Cor 10:10). Thus, keeping Christ and the cross at the heart of one's message is not at odds with effective communication. Instead, Paul is decrying the empty sophistry and verbal dexterity of Greek teachers who loved to debate points while paying no regard to the truth. It is possible that some members of the Corinthian church were attracted to such speaking arts; Paul was not.

Question 2. This is a difficult subject. It partly hinges on whether there is a difference between being of the world and being worldly. Christians have greatly benefited from advances in printing, radio, television, computer networks and other modern forms of communication. God has used each of these to spread the gospel and build his church. However, along with technology the art and science of advertising and marketing have become increasingly sophisticated. When does using such tools of the world become worldly and a subversion of the gospel? Ask the group!

Question 3. The wisdom of this age is available to everyone through investigation, research or experience. But such methods can tell us nothing about God's thoughts and plans. God's wisdom remains absolutely hidden from us unless God chooses to reveal himself to us. Paul claims that God has, in fact, revealed himself by his Spirit.

Verse 9 is a quote from Isaiah 64:4. *Mystery* (note especially Ephesians) or *secret wisdom* (v. 7) in the New Testament refers to the revealed truth of the gospel, the good news of God as Savior, and not to some special esoteric knowledge. At the heart of God's wisdom lies the crucifixion (v. 8). It is crucial (pun intended) to understand that the cross thus lies at the heart of mature discipleship (1:17; 2:2). As we will see, standing in contrast to a lot of immature Corinthian spirituality are individual lives and whole churches shaped around the cross.

Questions 6 & 8. Paul sees all of humanity as divided into those who have the Spirit (Christians) and those who do not (non-Christians). Yet not all those who have the Spirit are "spiritual," as Paul indicates in 3:1-4. This may be surprising and sobering to some group members and a source of lively discussion as to the implications for Christian fellowship and discipleship. A spiritual Christian is a "mature" Christian (2:6) as opposed to an "infant" (3:1). Those who are spiritually mature can eat "solid food" (that is, understand God's cross-shaped wisdom) whereas infants can only drink "milk" (the elementary truths of the gospel).

Unfortunately, the Corinthians were not spiritually mature. Although they had the Spirit, their spiritual growth had been stunted through disobedience (3:4). Paul calls them "worldly" (3:1)—those whose actions and understanding were infantile even though they had known Christ for some years.

Question 7. In reference to verse 15, care is required to avoid concluding that believers are above all forms of judgment from others, including non-Christians. In the moral sphere believers are very open to outside criticism and correction, as Paul himself demonstrates in chapters 5 and 6. Yet Paul knows that a life lived through and for the gospel will not always be understood by those without the Spirit. Nevertheless, we are to be faithful witnesses to the gospel as God leads us, prayerfully expecting the Spirit to open the hearts of our non-Christian friends.

Study 3. 1 Corinthians 3:5-23. Founded on Christ.

Purpose: To discover various pictures of a growing church and thereby gain a biblical perspective on human leadership in God's plan.

Group discussion. A large board or piece of chart paper would aid the group tallying. Do not spend time debating the clarity or validity of this exercise (any intense desire to argue about it would itself be revealing and perhaps worthy of discussion!). The most important thing is to get at and be warned about the feelings that come from being marginalized or elevated in any way.

Question 1. The group may have difficulty with this question at first. Help them to see that Paul compares himself and Apollos to farmers (vv. 6-9) and builders (vv. 10-15). He likewise compares the church to God's field (v. 9), God's building (v. 9) and God's temple (v. 16). Don't worry about the details of these metaphors at this point since they will be covered later in the study.

Question 2. In the first part of this question, be sure to look not only at the field but also at the workers in the field. Explore how apt this agricultural metaphor is for the church.

Question 4. Notice that there is a master builder (Paul), a foundation (Jesus Christ), building materials (gold, silver, wood), other builders (ministers like Apollos and Cephas) and a day when the owner of the building will judge the quality of the construction.

Question 5. Using an image that spans the centuries, Paul pictures a fire raging through a city, hardly touching masonry buildings but consuming wooden and grass shacks, with the builder of such flimsy structures barely escaping "like a man pulled to safety through the smoke and flames of his burning house" (F. F. Bruce, *1 and 2 Corinthians* [London: Marshall, Morgan & Scott, 1978], p. 44).

The image of fiery judgment may cause some Christians to question their salvation because they are so aware of being poor witnesses or of having failed in some Christian service. The builder's salvation is not in question, for that is by God's grace, but rather the "reward" (vv. 8, 14) of having built something of lasting value that will survive God's judgment.

Question 6. Throughout 1 Corinthians it is amazing to observe that God's salvation, presence and gifts are not dependent on our maturity or obedience but rather on his grace.

Question 7. People often assume that Paul is speaking of destroying the temple of our bodies through such things as smoking, drinking and so on. But the temple Paul refers to here is not our bodies (as in 1 Cor 6:19) but the church as a whole. Likewise, the destruction he has in mind is not individual but corporate.

The church as God's building, built on "the stone" (Is 28:16), is not something we break; we break ourselves against it. As a Pharisee persecuting the church, Paul himself had found that it is hard "to kick against the goads" (Acts 26:14, "goad" being a sharp stick). In the same way, he will soon mention how some community-destroying persons in Corinth had hurt themselves by failing to discern their relationships within the body of Christ (1 Cor 11:30).

Question 9. God has given us everything in Christ. Unfortunately, the NIV obscures the parallel between 1:12 and 3:21-23 by the translation "I follow Paul" rather than "I belong to Paul" (RSV), which is implied by the Greek. The idea of belonging (as well as union) is also implied by the statements "You are of Christ, and Christ is of God" (3:23).

The ground is level before the cross. No matter what our background, education, income or position in the church, we are all simply servants of God. The world calls this holy egalitarianism foolishness, but it is God's wisdom in community building.

Now or Later. In this chapter, Paul is thinking primarily of building the Christian community. But throughout his letters Paul teaches that our calling embraces all of life. Vocation is not only the work of the ministry but the ministry of work! It is not only building the house of God, but building one's family for God. Whether we work for God in so-called secular society or in the Christian community, we serve the same God for the same reason with the same motivation.

Study 4. 1 Corinthians 4. Servants of Christ.

Purpose: To challenge people to become fools for Christ, with eyes fixed on eternal glory.

Question 1. This question is fairly easy to answer, so don't dwell on it. Move on to question 2.

Question 2. Our faithfulness comes in reflecting God's character as revealed in Christ, the ultimate servant. How did he think and act? Faithfulness also implies consistency and dependability. God is marked supremely by faithfulness (1:9).

Question 3. Christians today often make the same mistakes as the Corinthians. We judge on the basis of appearance, personality, academic degrees, number of study guides authored(!), speaking ability, prestige, success and so on.

Question 4. Paul is unconcerned about the judgment of others, whether those in the world or in the church, and he is hesitant to judge himself. Yet some qualifications of this position are immediately necessary.

First, if any judgment was appropriate, it must be applied by spiritual people with criteria shaped not by the world but by the secret things of God (4:1), that is, the gospel (compare 2:15).

Second, Paul is not declaring himself perfect. Verse 4 may be translated "I am conscious of nothing against myself, yet I am not by this acquitted" (NASB). He simply does not feel he or anyone else is qualified to judge in this particular circumstance.

Third, the circumstance is *specific.* Paul is not saying he is above the assessment of the community or of introspection when it comes to moral issues (see 1 Cor 5:3, 12; 11:31 to prove this point). The question here is not morality but rather the manner and motive of ministry. In this regard Paul is adamant—only the Lord is capable of judging motives and giving rewards. With an eye fixed on eternal judgment, Paul's only concern is to be a faithful servant.

Question 6. The mention of Apollos here and again (perhaps with frustration) in 16:12 and the absence of any evidence that Cephas (Peter) actually visited Corinth makes it likely that the Apollos party was in fact Paul's main source of grief. These were folks who had forgotten that all leaders were given to them as a gift from God (see 3:22). Therefore, it was highly inappropriate to elevate one leader over another. Even more, the style and content of wisdom which they may have prized in Apollos was either worldly or (quite possibly) a gift of God in Christ (see again 1:5). In either case it was no ground for boasting in men. It is good to know that Titus 3:13 suggests a happy ending in the relationship between Paul and Apollos.

Questions 8-10. Paul's words only make sense in light of the concept of suffering coming before glory. Scripture teaches this perspective on life and suffering for Christ, for example, in Romans 8:17-39. The Bible affirms that having suffered, Christ now reigns in glory (Col 3:1). We too will reign with him in glory at his return (Col 3:4) provided we share in his sufferings now (Rom 8:17).

The Corinthians, however, wanted to have the glory now and skip the suffering. Or perhaps more accurately, they assumed that suffering was a sign of weakness and a lack of God's blessing. Therefore, they had no alternative but to conclude that Paul must be a poor example of a Christian and an apostle. Paul stands this kind of thinking on its head!

As the group contrasts the Corinthians' experiences with those of Paul and the apostles, be sure to notice the vivid language Paul uses. The group should try to imagine what Paul is describing. He is thinking of the gladiatorial contests in the Roman arena, or perhaps the triumphal parade of a victorious Roman general. The Christians are on display at the end of the procession and are brought into the arena to die. The whole universe, including the angels, is "in the stands" watching this spectacle.

The passage is rich in irony—the use of words to express something other than the literal meaning, usually pointing to an incongruity between perception and reality. There is the irony that the Corinthians believe they have become spiritual "kings"; the irony that Paul and the other apostles most deserving of honor are in fact treated as the scum of the earth; and finally, the irony that being a sacrificial servant of Christ and his gospel may cause us to be viewed as fools in the eyes of the world (and even of arrogant members of the church), but that same service will one day lead to glory.

The deepest irony in this paragraph is that the Corinthians have not yet learned that the only way to the front of the procession is to serve at the end of it. Thus they may appear wise next to Paul. They may think themselves superior, but in the end the foolish apostle, condemned to die, is the one on the royal road. Of course, this is the same road that his Lord walked before him; and note (especially in v. 12) that it is the kind of road mapped out in the Sermon on the Mount.

Question 12. The group should answer the second question twice, first with regard to the Corinthians and then with regard to their own thoughts and actions.

Now or Later. Paul may be referring to ecstatic speech and other signs and wonders. However, in light of the first four chapters this seems unlikely (see, for example, 1:22). It is much more likely that Paul is thinking in 4:20 of the power of the cross as a sign of the kingdom—a power made evident in the sacrificial servanthood of his ministry. Thus a whip is not the necessary symbol of power. There are a lot of themes in this chapter that tie together the previous three. For example, Paul knows that a spirit of love and humility can break the stoniest of hearts. So it is when one comes in weakness and fear and trembling that God's power is revealed (2:3, 5). This is the kind of "wise folly" that the Corinthians needed to learn (3:18). As Paul wrote them in a later epistle, "That is why, for Christ's sake, I delight in weaknesses, in insults, in hardships, in persecutions, in difficulties. For when I am weak, then I am strong" (2 Cor 12:10).

Study 5. 1 Corinthians 5—6. Members of Christ.
Purpose: To grasp the importance of corporate and personal purity.
Question 1. In Greece there was no shame in having sexual relationships before marriage or outside of marriage. Demosthenes writes, "We keep mistresses for pleasure, concubines for the day-to-day needs of the body, but we have wives in order to produce children legitimately and to have a trustworthy guardian of our homes

The NIV uses the words "sexual immorality" (v. 1) for the Greek *porneia*. *Porneia* is a general word for unlawful sexual behavior ranging from sexual relationships before marriage to sexual relationships outside of marriage. One of the few Old Testament regulations imposed on Gentile Christians, who lacked a Jewish moral and religious heritage, was this ban on fornication (Acts 15:29; 21:25). It has been said that the one virtue that the church gave to the ancient world was chastity.

That a man should cohabit with his stepmother, even if she was younger than him, was forbidden by Old Testament law (Lev 18:8; Deut 22:30; 27:20; see 2 Sam 20:3). Old Testament examples of such outrageous fornication are found in Genesis 35:22; 49:4; 2 Samuel 16:22; and 1 Chronicles 5:1.

Question 2. Handing this person "over to Satan" probably means to expel him from the community where Jesus is confessed as Lord into the secular realm where Satan dominates (Mt 18:17-19; 1 Tim 1:20). But Paul adds the important qualifying purpose: "That the sinful nature [*sarx* or "flesh"] may be destroyed and his spirit saved on the day of the Lord" (v. 5). Either Paul is prophesying a physical sickness as God's disciplinary punishment of this man (as in 11:30, 32), or he is intending that exclusion from the Christian community would result, eventually, in repentance (crucifying the sinful nature) and true spiritual life before God. In either case Paul's desire is that the person be saved, not damned. Ultimately, he is aiming not at exclusion but rather inclusion in the community of faith, but only on terms that promote spiritual health for the individual and the whole church.

Question 3. Many people have heard or experienced examples of disastrous and usually unwarranted church discipline. In reaction they want no part in church discipline and would rather tolerate a gross and persistent sin than risk losing the offender. (In all honesty, the reticence about discipline often has more to do with the frustration and embarrassment of losing someone not from the kingdom but to another congregation, where they easily can end up in these days of fluid church membership. Another fear is being criticized for not handling discipline perfectly or without pain, as if such things were possible when dealing with the human heart.) It will be important to guide people to notice how Paul, in spite of the practical and emotional complexities of discipline, challenges the church for not taking sin seriously even more than he brings the immoral individual to task. A living church requires an environment of "tough love" where each instance of wickedness will be handled proactively but sensitively. This is not an optional part of church life.

Question 5. The Corinthians practiced an odd kind of separation. Ironically, they tolerated gross sin within their fellowship while having as little possible contact with sinners outside the church! Paul shows that freedom in Christ gives one the courage to deal with sin *within* the community while having genuine relationships with people *outside* the community—yet without conforming to their lifestyle. You may want to focus as a group on what priority you are putting on friendships in the world. In keeping yourself from the world, are you also keeping the gospel and Christ's love from where it is most needed?

Question 6. The group by now may be getting thoroughly confused about the various judgment references in Corinthians. To clarify: "Judging the world" (6:2) is not guidance for our attitude and behavior toward a specific individual outside the church (see 5:12) but instead is a reference to the end of history. Likewise, "we will judge angels" (6:3) may refer to the fact that those associated with the Son of Man (Jesus) will share his ultimate reign over the earth (Dan 7:22), or it could refer to our share in Christ's victory over disobedient angels (Jude 6)—or to both. Christians can hardly be fit to share Christ's ultimate rule and judgment if they resort to pagans to settle their disputes. "As in the preceding matter [5:1-13], the heavier artillery is aimed at the community itself for allowing such a thing to happen" (Gordon D. Fee, *The First Epistle to the Corinthians* [Grand Rapids, Mich.: Eerdmans, 1987], p. 229). Although in this case the individual plaintiff also comes under fire for pressing his complaint. Commenting on Paul's restatement in verse 7 of the principle of nonretaliation taught by Jesus (Mt 5:39-42), T. W. Manson suggests that Paul is making two points: first, that Christian cases should at least be tried by Christian courts and second, that there should be no such cases! (*Studies in the Gospels and Epistles* [Manchester, U.K.: Manchester University Press, 1962], p. 198.) The issue is not only, as in 5:1-13, protection of the Christian community for its own sake but also in its reputation before the world (6:6). In both 5:1-13 and 6:1-8, the key to honoring the name of Christ and his followers is the proper exercise of discipline within the community.

Question 7. To see how the topic of going to court in other ways fits very well here in the letter, recall that public disputes within churches frequently revolve around financial and other resources (for example, Acts 6:1; 1 Cor 11:17-22). What is the similarity between sexual immorality and the possessiveness, resentment, and self-justification that often arise around money matters? Note that in the list of verses 9 and 10, greed appears right alongside sexual immorality. Both expressions involve a kind of defrauding of another (v. 8). It is sobering, given the hierarchy of sins that churches sometime maintain (with fornication at the top), that cheating in material ways is treated as seriously as sexual sin (see 11:20-22; 32-34).

Question 8. Paul warns us against being deceived because we are so easily deceived about this. After all, salvation is by grace, not by works, and Jesus came to save sinners. What does it matter (we think) if sinners keep on sinning? But such thinking overlooks the fact that a new life in Christ results in a new lifestyle (v. 11).

The sins listed refer to a continuous lifestyle or practice and not to a one-time involvement. Paul's list is similar to the works of the flesh in Galatians 5:19-21 (see also Eph 5:5). In each case, *persisting* in fleshly living is implied.

Likewise, Paul's mention of both "male prostitutes" and "homosexual offenders" does not mean that a person with a homosexual tendency who is living chastely is excluded from the kingdom. The two words Paul uses here, *malakoi* (men or boys who allow themselves to be misused homosexually) and *arsenokoitai* (a male homosexual, pederast, sodomite) both have an active meaning. They refer to behaviors and to attitudes that tolerate or promote such behaviors.

Question 10. Paul uses a number of arguments to refute the idea that "everything is permissible for me": (1) He states that although everything is permissible, not everything is beneficial (v. 12). (2) In contrast to the Greek idea that the body is the prison of the soul, Paul claims that God will resurrect our bodies just as he raised Jesus from the dead (v. 14). Bodily existence has eternal value. (3) He emphasizes that our bodies are members of Christ and should be treated accordingly (vv. 15-17). (4) In quoting the creation account of Genesis 2:24 Paul elevates sexual union with another to a serious spiritual and psychological level, which allows no casualness about such encounters (v. 16). Even more serious than the bits we may pick up (viruses) are the bits of ourselves we leave behind in "casual sex" or otherwise engaging in sex with many partners, even ones we may be married to for a time (what could be referred to as "serial polygamy"). (5) In contrast to other sins, Paul claims that sexual sins are committed against our own bodies (v. 18). (6) Paul states that our bodies are temples of the Holy Spirit and should be treated as holy (v. 19). (7) He stresses that our bodies are not our own but have been purchased by God and belong to him (v. 20).

Separately and together these provide powerful reasons for honoring God with our bodies (v. 20). It is arguments such as these that account for the strong tone Paul takes against the incestuous offender in 5:3 and for purity in all its forms throughout this and his other epistles.

Question 13. The Passover and the Feast of Unleavened Bread which followed it were annual remembrances of Israel's miraculous deliverance from Egypt (Ex 12). During this festival all the old leaven was removed from the house in order to make a clean start and to remember the unleavened bread they made while escaping from Egypt.

Question 14. According to John's Gospel, Jesus was crucified while the Passover lambs were being slain, a powerful statement of the new exodus he accomplished. Paul implies that the Passover lamb has been slain for the Corinthians, but God's house (the Christian community) has not been cleansed of the old yeast of malice and wickedness (v. 8). Objective salvation requires subjective cleansing. But how is this to be applied to a church practically? If every instance of sin required expulsion, every church building would be empty!

Question 15. There is a vast difference between those who are seeking to overcome their sin and those who embrace it and refuse to repent. The former description would apply to every Christian, whereas the latter would apply to those whom Paul would put out of the church. The issue often is the "teachability" of the person and the direction in which they are moving.

What about the fact that Paul called the Corinthians "worldly" and immature (3:1)? Why not put them out of the church as well? It is true that Paul used these words to describe the Corinthians, but that was because of their pride, quarreling and inability to understand the "solid food" in God's Word. However, we must balance this description with Paul's claim that the Corinthians no longer lived as they did as non-Christians (6:11). They still had a long way to go, but they had changed in many ways. There was evidence that they were on the right track. Unfortunately, people today often apply the label of "worldly" or "carnal" Christian to those whom Paul would not consider Christians at all! Unfortunately, instead of welcome, patience and fellowship, a more categorical "whip" is needed where a mockery is being made of the name of Christ.

Study 6. 1 Corinthians 7. Devoted to Christ.

Purpose: To discover how our devotion to Christ should affect our views of singleness, sex and marriage. Paul does not give us in this chapter a complete theology or handbook of marriage. He is dealing with specific issues out of which we must "mine" timeless truths.

Question 1. "It is good for a man not to marry" (v. 1 NIV) is not in quotation marks like "all things are lawful" (6:12 RSV). Some commentators feel it is a quotation from a letter delivered to Paul from Corinth rather than Paul's inspired word. Others believe it is Paul's own statement on the subject. In either case, Paul doesn't refute the statement but rather discusses why it may not be "good" for most people to refrain from marriage.

Different translations may confuse the exact issue Paul is addressing. The RSV and KJV follow the original Greek literally by saying "not to touch a woman." The NIV translates this as "not to marry" because the exact meaning of the word is to touch in sexual intercourse (see Prov 6:29). Some feel that Paul considers the matter only from the male point of view ("have no physical contact with women," Phillips), but we will soon discover how Paul was equally concerned about the purity, health and fulfillment of women, a remarkable thing for the era in which he was writing.

Paul's use of "gift" (v. 7) may lead to significant confusion. Some may think that celibacy (the single life) is a special capacity given by God (like a "gift of teaching") that makes it easy to be single. But in Paul's correspondence, "gift" is literally a "gracelet," a favor freely bestowed by God (William F. Arndt and F. Wilbur Gingrich, *A Greek-English Lexicon of the New Testament* [Chicago: University of Chicago Press, 1957], p. 878). Being able to remain contentedly single is not the result of having little natural desire or capacity for marriage (though Jesus alluded to this in Mt 19:11-12), or even of some supernatural transformation. As Paul understands it, remaining contentedly single or contentedly married both require grace, an active and continuous empowerment. Here, as elsewhere, devotion to Christ overrides what is natural or easy (Mt 19:12).

Question 2. In verse 2 Paul mentions that "there is so much immorality." At one time there were over one thousand sacred prostitutes to Aphrodite (goddess of love) in the temple in Corinth. However, the sexual attitudes and temptations in Corinth were not much different than those people face today.

Paul's practical advice that "each man should have his own wife, and each woman her own husband" (v. 2) may not seem so practical to those who would like to get married but for whatever reason cannot. If there are singles in your group, you may wish to discuss what Paul does not cover here: How can singles who do not have Paul's "gift" avoid sexual immorality if they have no immediate prospects for marriage?

Question 3. Using the word *duty* (v. 3) Paul describes marital obligations the same way he does the obligation to pay taxes (Rom 13:7)! In verse 4 he also uses the Greek word for "authority" or "right" (*exousia*) to describe the right or power each spouse has over the other's body. However, Paul's emphasis is on a radical self-giving rather than a selfish spouse-taking.

Some may be offended at this seeming sexual imperialism. But it is important to note that sexual submission in this chapter is *mutual*: the wife has equal rights to her husband's body, just as the husband has rights to his wife's body.

Question 4. Many groups today have someone who is separated or divorced.

Almost every group has children of divorced parents. Pastoral sensitivity is needed in approaching these questions without compromising Scripture. A compassionate heart is the key to accepting people who have broken God's Word or who are victims of life in a fallen world.

Paul quotes the words of the Lord Jesus, referring probably to Mark 10:2-12, especially the statement "what God has joined together let not man separate" (v. 9). Jesus used the same word "separate" or "leave" (*chōrizetō*) that Paul chose in 1 Corinthians 7:10, 15.

Many think this passage teaches two options for a seemingly hopeless marriage: separation of bed and board (without divorce), and divorce. But the Bible does not envisage a separation that is not a divorce. If there is no intercourse, no living together (v. 12), there is no marriage. However, the reverse is not true; that two people who have slept together (or "lived together" in modern terms) are married is definitely not what Paul teaches here (but note 6:16—extramarital intercourse may not produce true marriage, but it certainly creates problems for any future marriage).

When Paul writes in verse 11, "A husband must not divorce [*aphienai*] his wife," he uses another word, *aphiēmi*, which means to "send away in the legal sense of divorce" or "to dismiss one's spouse." Jewish society regulated very liberally the rights of a husband to divorce his wife. Some rabbis interpreted Deuteronomy 24:1 to mean that a man could divorce his wife if he now found her unattractive! But the Jewish woman could not divorce her husband, as opposed to Roman custom, which gave such rights to women. But Jesus and Paul took all such "rights" away from men and women in favor of a higher right, the power and possibility of living for God in the place of life you are in when God calls you (vv. 17, 20).

Paul's statement "but if she does" (v. 11) considers the possibility that a (presumably believing) woman might take the initiative to separate and divorce. In this case she is not "free" to remarry because she has broken the marriage covenant. She must remain unmarried or be reconciled.

Question 6. The biblical "grounds" for permissible divorce make for hot discussion. The evangelical consensus is that there are two permissible grounds for divorce that give the right to remarry: adultery by one's partner (not oneself) and desertion by the unbelieving spouse. However, in spite of a general consensus, many evangelicals hold a variety of views on divorce and remarriage, including the following: (1) Divorce is not allowed under any circumstances. (2) Divorce is allowed for sexual immorality or desertion of an unbelieving partner, but remarriage is not permitted. (3) Divorce and remarriage are allowed for sexual immorality or desertion by an unbelieving partner. (4) Divorce and remarriage are allowed for a variety of reasons.

Obviously it is not possible for the group to research all of the relevant passages in this study. It is important, therefore, to focus on Paul's concerns in this passage rather than trying to answer more questions than he is addressing.

Realize, too, that Paul's concern was not to regulate permissible divorce but to maintain healthy spirituality in believers, even in a mixed marriage. Since groups tend to focus on the rules of divorce, it will be important to stay with the concern of the text: being devoted to the Lord whether married or single, whether "happily" married or not.

Question 8. Paul has already affirmed the holiness of married life and the marriage bed. He has emphasized the spiritual influence a believer may have with an unbelieving partner (vv. 14, 16). Now by emphasizing the advantages of the single life he shows that the single person lacks nothing in being a complete Christian. Sexual fulfillment is not necessary. Your group may wish to discuss the appropriateness of celebrating someone's decision to remain single just as we now celebrate the announcement of someone's engagement!

"Virgins" (*parthenoi*, v. 25) probably refers to a special class of unmarried women, to be distinguished from unmarried women in general (*agamos*). The issue may have been whether women who were betrothed virgins should proceed to marriage in the normal way just because they were pledged to someone. In this chapter, however, Paul has both male and female celibacy in mind.

It is frequently argued that Paul's teaching in this chapter (especially vv. 25-35) was determined by "this present crisis" (v. 26) and therefore does not apply to all times and all situations. However, Paul offers some powerful reasons for radical devotion to Christ besides the "crisis" he refers to (however this may be interpreted). He says, for example, that "this world in its present form is passing away" (7:31), which emphasizes the transitoriness of everything secular in comparison with the certainty of Christ's kingdom. He says that married couples will have "troubles in this life" (7:28), and he wants to spare us this. He says that a married couple's interests are divided (v. 34), while he would like us to have undivided devotion to the Lord (v. 35). For Paul and for those who follow his teaching, it is not life now that sets the agenda but the kingdom and the King.

Question 9. Full covenant marriage in Genesis 2:24 requires three kinds of unity: "leaving" (public wedlock), "cleaving" (personal friendship) and "one flesh" (private consummation). Physical desire alone is an insufficient reason to be married. However, the high incidence of premarital sex in our society, even among Christians, calls for sensitive pastoral ministry. Many Christians hurry up their wedding because they are not able (or willing) to exercise self-control physically. Couples too involved physically have two better choices than a quick wedding: they can abstain physically for a time, submit to a process of forgiveness for the betrayal implied by all forms of premarital sex, and work on other levels of intimacy; or they can rely on the judgment of mature and experienced outsiders about their marriage readiness, and as a result of such counseling either break off or get married.

Question 10. 1 Corinthians 7:17-24 are some of the most difficult verses in the chapter partly because of confusing translations. The NIV accurately communicates that "called" in verses 17 and 20 is used in two senses: First, God has sovereignly assigned a place for every human being. Our life is not a series of accidents. Paul emphasizes this in verse 17: "Each one should retain the place in life that the Lord assigned to him and *to which God has called him.*" But this is not Paul's main use of called. In verse 20 he emphasizes rather that God's call to live in the kingdom of God (Eph 4:1; 1 Cor 1:26) comes to us *where we are:* "Each one should remain in the situation which he was in *when* God called him" (v. 20).

Both senses are needed to complete our understanding of Christian vocation (the word *vocation* simply means "calling"). God's call makes us be who we are where we are (a more static view promoting contentment and faithfulness). God's call also evokes kingdom living no matter who we are or where we are (a more dynamic view promoting discipleship and growth). "Never allow the thought—'I am of no use where I am'; because you certainly can be of no use where you are not" (Oswald Chambers, *My Utmost for His Highest* [New York: Dodd, Mead & Co., 1956], p. 291).

Study 7. 1 Corinthians 8—9. Living for Christ.

Purpose: To understand that living the gospel is more important than personal rights and freedoms, or even religious principles.

Group Discussion. This discussion of "rights" groups and movements should not degenerate into bashing or frivolous humor. The causes often have tragic roots, and each of them represent sensitive matters to some (including some in your own group).

Question 1. Paul clearly moves on to a new topic, another sparked by an inquiry from the Corinthians. There are at least two reasons why the issue of meat sacrificed to idols emerged at this point. First, the Corinthians may have had an uneasy conscience about whether animals slaughtered in pagan worship before idols became spiritually contaminated. They may also have wondered whether Christians should pursue independent butchering and meat preparation as the Jews did. Second, some in Corinth may have sought to apply the injunction of the Jerusalem council to "abstain from food polluted by idols" and "from the meat of strangled animals and from blood" (Acts 15:20).

Similarly, there are two reasons why the mature would be quite willing to eat idol meat. First, on the pragmatic side, much of the best meat available in the marketplace came straight from the many Corinthian temples, since only a token portion would be "received" by the deity, and the surplus could not be consumed by the priests and attendants alone. Second, on the spiritual side, the mature knew that neither idols nor rules about eating idol meat had any meaning next to the reality of the true God.

Question 2. Paul cautions the Corinthians against wounding another's conscience by their exercise of rights and freedoms. After all, a brother is of much greater value than food—greater even than our "rights." In particular, Paul has no patience with those who would push freedom beyond the marketplace and into the realm of accepting invitations to dinner parties often held in temples, under the nominal patronage of a pagan deity. Although meaningless to the one "with knowledge" (see 10:18-22), such behavior would have been scandalous to many of the Christians with scruples sensitized by past pagan experience (v. 7). Ultimately, Paul raises the stakes even higher, indicating that love for one's brother is very much connected with one's relationship to God (v. 3) and love for Christ (v. 12). This is the same teaching found everywhere in the New Testament (see, for example, 1 Jn 4:20-21).

Question 5. The comments on Paul's apostleship are very much in keeping with the topic of rights and freedoms as outlined in chapter 8. Paul spends the first half of the chapter establishing his apostolic rights. In the second half he explains why he does not claim any of his rights.

It is not exactly clear what lay behind the Corinthians' criticism of Paul's apostolic behavior. They may have felt that Paul's refusal to accept financial support from the church made him suspect. His refusal may have embarrassed the Corinthians, who wanted to be seen as able to provide for their leaders. Perhaps it caused Paul's position of authority to appear weaker than that of his rivals who, one assumes, were not reluctant to receive gifts.

Question 6. One of the first things people criticize about radio and TV preachers is their constant pleas for money. Unfortunately, such pleas make it easy for people to assume that the preacher is just trying to get rich. The same charge is sometimes leveled at local churches, especially those engaging in a building fund drive.

Question 8. Paul more than once demonstrated a willingness to engage in "holy compromise" for the sake of the gospel (Acts 15:22-30; compare Acts 16:3 and Gal 2:11-14). In the immediate context, Paul is willing to be "weak" by not eating idol meat if it upsets certain brothers and "strong" against those who would take their freedom too far by eating in idol temples. In all things Paul's guiding principle is to be a slave to Christ, to the gospel, and to those who need to hear it, not letting any disputable matter stand in the way (see Rom 14). Obviously, such a view requires us to distinguish the heart of the gospel from peripheral issues, which of course itself sometimes becomes the substance of the debate (one person's periphery is another person's center). Paul has given us some provocative guidelines to make such decisions in a way that is calculated to upset many dearly held beliefs in our traditional doctrines and methods of ministry.

Study 8. 1 Corinthians 10. Eating with Christ.
Purpose: To invite people to choose a life of freedom in Christ that is beneficial for themselves and others.
Questions 1-2. Paul sees parallels between Israel's spiritual experiences and those of the Corinthians. The Israelites were baptized in the cloud and sea and into (the leadership of) Moses, just as the Corinthians were baptized *in* water and *into* Jesus Christ. Paul's main point is that both groups were baptized, not precisely *how* they were baptized.

Likewise, the Israelites ate spiritual food *(manna)* and drank (water from the rock), just as the Corinthians ate the bread and drank the wine during the celebration of holy Communion.

However, Israel's spiritual experiences were no guarantee of protection against God's judgment. In spite of their experiences, God judged them because of their idolatry, sexual immorality, testing and grumbling. Likewise, the Corinthians (and we) should beware of sinning against the Lord lest God's judgment fall.

These questions may be confusing to members of the group who have very little understanding of the story of Israel's salvation and its significance as a parable of the believer's experience today. The leader should become familiar with these major events by reading about the golden calf (Ex 32:4-6) and the seduction of Israel by Moab (Num 25:1-9).

Paul's reference to drinking out of a rock, as a foretaste of knowing Christ, restates the story of Numbers 20:1-12. The "snakes" (1 Cor 10:9) were a response to grumbling (Num 21:4-7), with a raised bronze snake ultimately being a focus for healing faith—though Jesus, not Paul, makes this latter connection (Jn 3:14).

While few in the group will be able to systematize these wilderness experiences, all can profit from Paul's terse summary of their *meaning:* "These things occurred as examples to keep us from setting our hearts on evil things as they did." Make sure the group understands the intent of Paul's comparison. Just as the whole Israelite nation enjoyed God's blessing at the beginning of the journey, but only a few remained in these blessings, so it is possible that not all redeemed members of the Corinthian community will in the end enjoy Christ's blessing.

As this passage does not specifically deal with whether one can lose salvation, it is probably unprofitable to explore this subject here.

Questions 4-5. The Greek word for temptation means either a "trial" or "testing." Trials can come from God to produce maturity, just as temptations can come from Satan to make people fall. In these verses both meanings apply. God wanted the pressures of the surrounding pagan culture to be a means of spiritual growth, but Satan used these pressures to seduce believers into sin. Since God is ultimately in charge and marvelously available to believers (v. 13), the Corinthians have an escape. Make sure the group discovers that the escape is not *from* temptation but *in* it, through overcoming it in Christ's power.

Someone in the group may be able to illustrate how God turned a situation in which Satan seduced them toward sin into a trial that produced faith and righteousness. You need to be sensitive to persons who feel persistent failure before a repeated temptation or who unwisely put themselves into seductive situations that could never be positive trials. Most will easily think of sexual testing and temptations. It may be more useful and challenging to explore the temptations of greed and pride, which, as we saw in 1 Corinthians 6, are just as deadly.

Question 6. The reference to participating in a fellowship table with demons (v. 21) may spark some lively discussion. Paul's argument is very delicate. On the one hand, Paul sides with the "strong" in saying that an idol is no god at all and has no demonic influence (8:4-6). On the other hand, Paul realizes that the "weak" Christian feels the idol has a real existence and power (8:7). Therefore he also lovingly sides with the weak, warning of the danger of unwittingly yielding to the powers of darkness by trying to mix Christian and pagan worship or lifestyles. As always Paul holds up proactive loving as the main motivator (see v. 24), rather than winning theological debates. Remember, though Christians of tender conscience may be "weak," it is the quarreling Corinthians who are called "worldly" and immature (3:1).

The church fathers usually understood this passage to suggest that pagan worshipers sacrificed to particular demons. Some may wish to conclude from this that any involvement in Eastern religion today inevitably leads to demon possession. This, however, is more than Paul says. His concern is not to explain pagan idolatry but to win people to undivided participation in the life of Christ in the Spirit.

Question 7. Where the "rubber meets the road" on the doctrine of the Lord's Supper is not whether it is a sacrament or symbol but whether the worshiper truly participates in the death and resurrection of Christ. The person who has a "high" doctrine of the sacrament but lives immorally is practicing a heresy! Stay with what the text says. The table is a "participation" in the blood and body. The Greek word *koinonia* means "fellowship" and shared experience. Paul means no more or less!

Question 8. Again quoting and critiquing a slogan of the Corinthians (compare 6:12 and 10:23), Paul emphasizes that our "freedom" or our "rights" should not be our primary concern. Rather, he stresses that the following principles should guide our behavior: (1) Do only those things which are beneficial and constructive for yourself and others (v. 23). (2) Don't seek your own good (only), but the good of others (vv. 24, 33). (3) Realize that the earth is the Lord's and everything in it—including those things that some people consider spiritually contaminated or inherently evil (such as meat offered to idols, v. 26). (4) Don't do anything that will cause someone's conscience to condemn your freedom in Christ (vv. 28-30)—one way, at least, to understand these difficult verses (also see "Now or Later" below). (5) Don't do anything that will cause either non-Christians or Christians to "stumble" (v. 32). (6) Seek to bring the gospel to people in any way possible (v. 33). (7) Do everything for the glory of God (v. 31).

Note how the last two verses of the chapter, 32-33, neatly sum up the main teaching of chapters 8 and 9 respectively. Clearly, this entire portion of 1 Corinthians holds together. On the continuing issue of meat sacrificed to idols, first introduced at 8:1, see "Now or Later" below.

Question 9. Encourage members of the group to share their own "freedoms" which might cause someone else to stumble. In Eastern cultures (and missionary contexts) this is a day-by-day issue. In Western cultures, the principle finds application in less religious matters. Note that Paul's concern is not merely to keep everybody happy by conforming to the expectations of others (10:29-30). He is concerned not to offend the *conscience* of others and hinder their salvation, growth and discipleship. While Paul does not say so directly in this passage, he has a mission to the "strong" to make them more loving in practice and a mission to the "weak" to make them stronger in belief!

Now or Later. Paul's continuing argument about freedom and food "sold in the meat market" is complicated, but it all revolves around witnessing to the gospel in the end. Here are the salient points: (1) Paul restates the principle that even if meat has been dedicated to an idol, it can be made kosher simply by giving thanks to God (v. 30). This is a "strong" testimony to the freeing power of the gospel in order to be able to worship the true God and fully enjoy his creation. (2) This allows for the following application. While Paul forbids table fellowship with immoral church members (5:9-12), he does not discourage believers from having table fellowship with unbelievers, even though the Christians' consciences will be tested on such occasions. Paul's attitude here contrasts sharply with the strict Jewish attitude illustrated by Peter's words to Cornelius (Acts 10:28). Contact with unbelievers on their turf is fundamental to gospel work. (3) Finally, Paul seems to have in mind the situation where a pagan might say, "This has been offered in sacrifice" (v. 28) to embarrass the Christian, knowing that idolatry was offensive. During the persecutions of the Jews under Antiochus IV (2 Maccabees 6:7-11), refusing forbidden food was used as a test of faith. Similar "test cases" presented themselves to Christians in the Roman Empire. In such cases, Paul urged believers to refuse the food, not because it was sinful or in fear of judgment by people or by God, but in order to bear witness *according to the conscience of the host*. The risk of limiting one's freedom at this point is outweighed by the risk of limiting the impact of the gospel. How does one navigate through these different sensitivities to the gospel? Only by catching the wind of the Spirit!

Study 9. 1 Corinthians 11. Headship of Christ.

Purpose: To discover how we can honor God and each other during our worship.

Question 1. It is important to let people share the various possible answers to this question: the relationship between the sexes, authority, order and freedom, and the marriage relationship. All of these answers will give some clue to the passage and help a common interpretation to emerge later.

Question 2. Verse 3 is the center of a raging controversy in the modern church. Those who believe that men should be in authority over women (at least men acting as husbands in a marriage or as elders in a church) usually interpret head as "chief" or "ruler." Likewise, Christian feminists usually interpret it as "source" or "origin."

Some interpreters see a straight hierarchy in verse 3: God is over Christ, who is over man, who is over woman. For a good presentation of this view see James Hurley, *Man and Woman in Biblical Perspective* (Grand Rapids, Mich.: Zondervan, 1981), p. 166. However, it may be better to see verse 3 as a series of comparisons. Paul is not emphasizing "God over Christ over man over woman" but rather is saying that the Christ-human relationship is like the man-woman relationship, which is like the God-Christ relationship.

Comparing husband and wife with God the Father and Christ helps us understand headship as a priority within a relationship of equals. It has nothing to do with greater and inferior. In the mysterious economy of the Trinity, the Father has priority over the Son, but they are equal and one (Jn 10:30).

In this series of headship comparisons one common element is the matter of giving glory: the Father is glorified in the Son. Christ glorifies himself in his bride, the church. There is a special sense in which the wife brings glory to her husband by recognizing his place in her life (11:7).

Don't let the group discussion grind to a halt on verse 3—there is more to come! (A mediating position between headship as rule and no headship at all in Christian marriage is taken in R. Paul Stevens, *Married for Good* [Downers Grove, Ill.: InterVarsity Press, 1986], pp. 111-31.)

Question 3. Verse 4 involves wordplay: every man who prays or prophesies (that is, engages in public worship) with a covered head brings dishonor to his head, Jesus Christ (v. 3). Also, he brings confusion to his role in relationship to God (v. 7) and woman (vv. 8-10). We have to admit, along with Gordon Fee, that we may never know to what the hypothetical male head covering actually refers (*The First Epistle to the Corinthians* [Grand Rapids, Mich.: Eerdmans, 1987], p. 508). The important thing is that a symbol understood in Corinth to represent a theological reality is at stake.

Question 4. Since we have no cultural equivalent to veils to signal a right marital relationship, try imagining instead the confusion that would result in our own culture if men and women took off their wedding rings in church because some people said, "In Christ sexual differences and propriety mean nothing." According to *The IVP Bible Background Commentary: New Testament* (Craig S. Keener [Downers Grove, Ill: InterVarsity Press, 1993], p. 475), the background to Paul's concern about women is the clash of cultures between upper-class fashion, where women went unveiled to flaunt their hairstyles, and the lower-class concern about modesty, sexual propriety and respect for household honor and the sacredness of marriage (still prevalent in Eastern cultures today). It is interesting to note that class distinctions may also have played a part in the problems surrounding the Lord's Supper (11:18, 20-22).

In Greek culture, prostitutes and women convicted of adultery often had their heads shaved; going around uncovered, including testing out such practices within the newfound freedom of church life, was equated to this shame (see vv. 5-6).

Paul's statement "because of the angels" (v. 10) has been interpreted various ways. The most probable is that angels were considered guardians of the created order. Once again Paul feels it is essential to live with the tension of accepting both the way we were created as different, male and female, and the way we are redeemed to be interdependent and equal (vv. 11, 12). Paul also argues from public propriety (v. 13), nature (vv. 14, 15) and general church practice (v. 16).

Question 6. There are many possible frustrations in this study: How does a single woman or man signal right relationships with the other sex? What exactly is masculinity and femininity? Does God want us to uphold hurtful cultural stereotypes of male or female roles for the presumed good of fighting the tide towards androgyny? Some progress can be made by asking the group what they understand about the distinctiveness of each sex and how they have come to celebrate the contribution of both sexes to the body of Christ.

Question 8. The words "fallen asleep" (v. 30; see 15:18, 20) are a euphemism for death. As a result of taking the Lord's Supper in an unworthy manner, God's judgment had fallen on various members of the Corinthian community. This judgment had resulted in weakness, sickness and, in some cases, even death.

The threat of judgment has kept many sensitive believers from receiving the benefits of the Lord's Supper. They simply do not feel good enough! Ironically they are the very people worthy to come, if they cling to Christ and his mercy. In contrast, the self-righteous who have broken relationships do not take the trouble to examine themselves in the right way and ultimately condemn themselves. This examination centers on "recognizing the body of the Lord." Following 10:17 and the context of this passage, "body" is almost certainly a reference to the church. The body (and blood) of the Lord in Communion is only precious and effective in the measure to which we esteem the body of the Lord and all the members that make it up.

Question 12. Against the background of Genesis 1:26-27 ("In the image of God he created him; male and female he created them"), Paul cannot mean that only males reflect God. He carefully does not say that woman is man's "image and likeness." But he does say that a woman will be the "glory" of her husband when she stands in right relationship to him, which is Paul's concern in Corinth.

Study 10 1 Corinthians 12. Body of Christ.

Purpose: To explore the nature and purpose of spiritual gifts in the body of Christ.

Group discussion. Spiritual gifts are not entirely unrelated to natural abilities or talents and may sometimes be an extra anointing of a so-called talent (Rom 12:6-8). Every good thing comes from God. This may help members of the group include persons in the discussion who are not yet believers or who are confused about spiritual gifts. Have chart paper ready for summarizing individual results. A risky idea is to have the group give feedback after each member outlines his or her most significant gift contribution to the group. Sometimes people do not see themselves or their impacts very clearly.

Question 2. Paul is once again answering the Corinthians' questions. Paul does not repeat their question, but it may have been "Which spiritual gift is the most inspired?" or "What is the surest sign of the Holy Spirit?" In replying, Paul is well aware that both tongues (*glossolalia*—utterance in languages not normally used by the speaker) and prophecy were found in pagan religions. The priestess of Delphi and the fortune-telling slave girl of Acts 16:16 are examples. Paul does not attribute any of the gift ministries in Corinth to demonic or pagan sources, but he does affirm that ecstasy is not the mark of the presence of the Holy Spirit. At this early stage in the discussion it would be unwise to entertain a long debate on whether tongues speaking ceased with the end of the apostolic age. While there is nothing in Scripture which proves that any of these gifts are now obsolete, our concern is not for the vindication of one or more spiritual gifts but with understanding the source and goal of all spiritual gifts. True gifts come from the Spirit, and the true Spirit will always inspire speech that honors the true nature of Jesus (v. 3).

Question 4. Help members of your group see the big picture of this section rather than grinding to a halt trying to define "a word of knowledge," "prophecy" or "the interpretation of tongues." Paul's concern was that the Corinthians should not see themselves as a collection of individual Christians performing their own ministries but as integrated members of the body of Christ.

Question 6. F. F. Bruce's comments on this are helpful. "No member is less a part of the body than any other member: all are necessary. Variety of organs, limbs and functions is of the essence of bodily life. No organ can establish a monopoly in the body by taking over the functions of the others. A body consisting of a single organ would be a monstrosity" (*Corinthians*, p. 121).

At this early stage in the discussion someone may confess that even though they are a Christian there is no evidence in them of a spiritual gift. This passage assures us that gifts are not something added to the believer after salvation as a fruit of maturity but are the inheritance of every believer (12:6). An important clue to resolving this common dilemma of "I don't know what my gift is" comes in verse 1. "Spiritual gifts" (12:1) could be translated "spiritual persons," since *pneumatikon* suggests "persons endowed with spiritual gifts" (F. F. Bruce, *Corinthians*, p. 116). Many people can be helped by knowing that who they are is a gift to the body.

Questions 8-9. These questions touch the nerve of the passage, namely Paul's repeated call to interdependence in Christ, which he has been developing (chapter 8, in the exercise of freedom; chapter 9, in his personal renunciation of the rights of an apostle; chapter 10, in dealing with differing consciences; and chapter 11, in male-female relationships in the church and mutual consideration at the Lord's Supper). What makes for disunity is not diversity of expression but an arrogant, independent attitude often expressed (or secretly thought of) in terms of the presumed superiority of one's own ministry. This passage underlines that no one has a gift alone!

Hardly anyone enjoys thinking of him- or herself as a "weaker" (v. 22) or "unpresentable" part of the body, though some who have poor self-images in the Christian community feel this at an emotional level. Paul seems to be using weaker here in two senses: According to 1 Corinthians 1:26-29, some are weak according to human standards, lacking in wisdom, eloquence and social graces. In 1 Corinthians 8:7 and 9:22 Paul uses "weak" in the sense of morally or spiritually immature. Surprisingly, Paul says that such persons are crucial to the health of the body—not just because they demand more care, but because they *are* indispensable.

"Uncomely parts" (KJV) or "unpresentable" parts may refer to the sex organs or the organs of secretion which, though hidden, are vital. God has so designed the body that we give the greatest care to the most hidden and the weakest parts, thereby demonstrating "equal concern for each other" (v. 25). It is the inspired logic of true church life, even if it reverses the laws of human society.

Question 10. Some may propose that Paul is enumerating the *historical* sequence of gifting to the church. If this were the case, following Ephesians 3:5 and 4:11, one could suggest that the apostles and prophets founded the church, and then pastor-teachers built the church. But in 1 Corinthians 12:28 that would leave the church today in a "post-teacher" environment, exclusively focused on miracle-workers, a possibility Paul would reject as unhelpful and divisive.

More probably Paul is enumerating gifts in terms of importance. The apostles are eyewitnesses of Christ and founders of churches; prophets declare God's Word with immediate relevance to life situations; teachers instruct fellow believers in Christian faith and practice; workers of miracles demonstrate God's power; healers are regularly used to bring divine healing to the sick; helpers attend to practical care as a spiritual ministry; administrators have the helmsman-leadership gift for the church. Those who speak in tongues are those who are gifted to speak messages in languages not normal to the speaker which, when interpreted, will edify the body (14:13).

Question 11. Many groups plan a special evening once a season or year for affirming every member's contribution. Each person is bombarded by the group with statements that complete the sentence "I find God uses you in this group through . . ." This avoids categorizing people according to fixed gifts. An illustration or two from your present group, especially about a person whom you know feels inferior or not needed, may edify everyone and model an ongoing process of life together.

Question 12. The New Testament does not give us a methodology for getting spiritual gifts because it is God who orders the body and decides how each member should function. Motivation is important (how I want to serve God), but more important than desiring to express one's own gift (or potential gift) must be the desire for the health of the body.

Encouraging scriptural longings for the group or church will go a long way toward alleviating gift frustration and preoccupation with the worth of one's own contribution. Once again, gifts emerge in mutual life and ministry and are fractions of Christ's continuing ministry in a body-life context. No one can therefore properly speak of "my" gift!

Study 11. 1 Corinthians 13. Love of Christ.

Purpose: To discover how love in the Christian community is the greatest way to express interdependence in Christ.

Personal reflection. If you discuss this in your group, be aware that you may have members who are currently struggling with abuse from others and deep hurts. They will not easily speak of being loved. However, with some encouragement most people can find a significant "other" in their life, often in childhood, who communicated a measure of unconditional love.

Question 1. The major difficulty in leading a study on 1 Corinthians 13 is the hazard of overfamiliarity with the words and underfamiliarity with the message. Reading the passage in a fresh translation such as Today's English Bible or a paraphrase like that of Phillips or *The Message* may draw fresh meaning from the chapter.

Question 2. "A Christian community can make shift somehow if the 'gifts' of chapter 12 be lacking: it will die if love is absent" (F. F. Bruce, *Corinthians*, p.

124).

Steer the group discussion away from pointless introspection about loveless-ness toward objectively assessing the fruits of love in the community. For example, is your ministry a model of kindness that is proving to be infectious? **Question 3.** By suggesting that the group define each quality, we are trying to break the familiarity barrier with this passage. For example, "rude" (v. 5) also means behaving disgracefully or dishonorably. The unmarried person who insists on sexual relations because of his or her "love" would, if truly loving, respect the rights and honor of the beloved. The same vocabulary is used in 1 Corinthians 7:36 for similar indiscretion. In lesser matters, cour-tesy has been called "love in the trifles." Much ministry simply lacks basic courtesy.

Questions 4-5. It is hard to maintain balance in a discussion of love and gifts. On the one hand, gifts are important right now. But one day God will abolish prophecy, tongues and knowledge (v. 8). In the meantime we must abolish the childish thinking (v. 11) that the exceptional is the best. Gifts are great for the time being, but love is greater. Prophecy without love will do nothing to build up people or edify the body (13:2; 14:3), no matter how spiritual it is. This is difficult for some with a bent toward the prophetic to fully accept.

Question 6. In studying this passage it is important to keep Paul's long-term view. He is looking at the supremacy of love not only for now but forever. Faith will become sight, hope will become realization, but love remains in force eternally.

Question 7. The sources of disunity in Corinth may need to be reviewed: self-promoting leaders, exaltation of the ecstatic and sensational, envy and jealousy, grouping into cliques, and "freedom" gone wild. Each of these proves to be a disguised form of self-interest.

Love offers self-realization through self-surrender. Instead of saying, "I don't need you" (12:21) because you are different, love prizes others because of differences. Norman Wright defined love this way: "A person is in love with another individual when meeting the emotional needs of that person becomes an emotional need of his or her own life."

Study 12. 1 Corinthians 14. Speaking for Christ.

Purpose: To explore the place of inspired speech in the Christian community.

General note. In this study we enter deep and troubled waters for many peo-ple in the church. The attitude toward tongues and prophecy as gifts of the Spirit has been varied and controversial in church history. The lines have usu-ally been drawn between those of a "Pentecostal" or "charismatic" persuasion and those sometimes called "traditional" or "conservative."

Some favor the continuation or revival of certain gifts of ecstatic or extemporaneous speech in congregational meetings. Others tend to downplay the importance of both tongues and prophecy and, in some cases, interpret 1 Corinthians 13:8 to mean that we now live in an age that has moved beyond these manifestations.

Some objections to tongues and prophecy today come from (1) a fear of or personal aversion to the nonrational, subjective or intuitive side of religion; (2) a distrust of any overemphasis or even tolerance of certain bizarre and undisciplined practices; (3) an abhorrence of the theology which claims that tongues is the necessary mark of a second blessing known as Spirit baptism; (4) a tendency toward elitism and perfectionism in some who use these gifts; (5) a desire to avoid the divisions which can follow the introduction of so-called charismatic gifts (including healing, miracles, and words of wisdom and knowledge) into body life.

All we can ask in this one study in one (long) chapter of 1 Corinthians is that, as far as possible, the participants put aside their traditions and prejudices and even previous experiences and open themselves freshly to the message Paul has for us.

There has been considerable debate surrounding how we should define tongues and prophecy. For the sake of this study we will define *both* tongues and prophecy as gifts of inspired, unplanned utterances in a Christian meeting, the former coming to the speaker in an unknown language and the latter in a known language. It is widely acknowledged that inspired preaching has some of the same prophetic dimensions of immediacy, directness and anointing from God, even though it usually is the fruit of careful preparation.

Question 1. Apparently the Corinthians had elevated the gift of tongues to a much higher status than prophecy as a mark of the Christian leader, perhaps because it seemed more spiritual and "otherworldly" than speech with understandable content.

Paul has a relatively low view of the usefulness of tongues in congregational meetings because the gift fails to build up the body. However, his remarks apply only to uninterpreted tongues. When tongues were interpreted in the meeting, the speech was equivalent to prophecy, and people were edified.

There are only hints concerning Paul's understanding of the relationship between prophecy in a local church and other revelation that has more permanent and universal force. Paul raises one standard above all speech in public assemblies, namely the discerning gifts of the corporate body (v. 29), which presumably rely on the abiding truth of the "word of God" (v. 36). These Old Testament Scriptures, together with "the Lord's command" which came to the Corinthians through the apostles' preaching and teaching (v. 37), have come down to us today in the Bible. This ultimate controlling rule over congregational word ministry has not been superseded by Paul and should not be by us.

Question 3. Our worship is meaningless or mindless when, for example, we sing hymns without paying attention to their content, or listen to sermons without applying their messages, or take Communion without reflecting on its meaning.

Question 4. God used the foreign language of the invading Assyrians as a sign to unbelieving Israel that God's judgment was coming on them (Is 28:11, 12). Paul concludes from this that tongues are a sign to unbelievers. Prophecy, on the other hand, is directed toward those who believe and are open to obeying God's Word.

There is an apparent contradiction between Paul's statement about the purpose of tongues and prophecy (v. 22), and his illustration about the effect of these gifts on an unbelieving visitor (vv. 23-25). This conundrum prompted the famous Bible translator, J. B. Phillips, to give up on finding an exegetical solution: "This is the sole instance of the translator's departing from the accepted text. He felt bound to conclude, from the sense of the next three verses, that we have here either a slip of the pen on the part of Paul, or, more probably, a copyist's error" (*The New Testament in Modern English* [London: Collins, 1960], p. 552).

A better solution is to see that the apostle, oblivious to the ambiguity that would cause later interpreters so much trouble, is simply saying two different things in these verses: (1) tongues *are* for unbelievers in the sense that they are a sign of stubborn unbelief and rebellion (consistent with Jesus' teaching on parables, Mt 13:11-15), and (2) tongues are *not* for unbelievers in the sense that such unintelligible speech will seem strange to unbelieving visitors in the church meeting.

Questions 5-7. There is a parallelism in verses 27-34 which is clear in Greek and in some English translations if one highlights the words *speak* (vv. 27, 29, 34) and *be silent* (vv. 28, 30, 34). The NIV has drawn out this parallelism by translating the word "speak" *(laleō)* the same way in all three verses. But it has obscured the other half of the parallelism by translating the word "be silent" *(sigaō)*—which is also the same in all three verses—in three different ways: "keep quiet" (v. 28), "stop" (v. 30), and "remain silent" (v. 34). Paul is telling the Corinthians (1) when those with the gift of tongues should speak and be silent; (2) when prophets should speak and be silent; and (3) when women should speak and be silent.

Question 7. This question could be very controversial for some in your group. However, confusion will be minimized if the group considers the following.

Your first goal should be to understand what Paul is saying in this passage, since it is the one being studied. You should avoid bringing in other passages prematurely.

After you feel you have a basic grasp of this passage, you can then compare Paul's teaching here with what he said in chapter 11 (study 9), a passage you have studied previously. This may cause you to modify your interpretation of one passage or the other.

You should realize that one's view of women's ministries should not be based on these two passages alone. Rather, a thorough study should be made (at a later time) of all the relevant texts. However, it is humbling to realize that even those who have studied all the texts often disagree about their interpretation. If everything were clear and unambiguous, there would be no controversy!

Now or Later. The group may wish to compare the typical worship service in Corinth with the typical worship service in their church. Although the former is not necessarily normative, we should be open to learn from the model described by Paul.

Study 13. 1 Corinthians 15—16. Hope in Christ.

Purpose: To have the hope of our resurrection become a powerful motivation in our lives.

Question 1. Although Christ's death (and burial) is obviously critical to our salvation from sin, Paul establishes the resurrection of Christ as the ultimate validation of his preaching and of his listeners' faith and forgiveness.

The possible distaste of some Corinthians over the thought of the actual physical burial and resurrection of Christ's body would have arisen from a general abhorrence of the physical and an elevation of the spiritual dimension of reality, including the notion of the "spiritual resurrection" of Christ.

Paul lists himself as the final eyewitness of the risen Christ (though abnormally so, as his encounter was the only postascension appearance of Christ), presumably referring to the Damascus road experience. We have no independent details of the appearances to five hundred brethren or to James, the Lord's brother.

Question 2. Paul lists the following consequences: "not even Christ has been raised" (v. 13), "our preaching is useless" (v. 14), "so is your faith" (v. 14), we are "false witnesses" (v. 15), "your faith is futile" (v. 17), "you are still in your sins" (v. 17), "those also who have fallen asleep in Christ are lost" (v. 18), "we are to be pitied more than all men" (v. 19).

Question 3. "Fallen asleep" (vv. 18, 20) is obviously an apt metaphor for death. It refers to the temporary nature of death rather than to the gentleness of death. Many are violently martyred for Christ, more today than ever in history.

"Firstfruits" (v. 20) refers to the first sheaf of the harvest that was given to the Lord—a token of the larger harvest that would follow.

Question 4. It should be noted that the second part of verse 22 is not universalistic; the next verse clearly restricts the ones "made alive" to "those who belong to him."

Question 5. For those who believe in annihilation upon death, the philosophy of verse 32 is logically and psychologically consistent, as suggested by the Preacher in Ecclesiastes 2:24. However, the rejection of the resurrection by the Corinthians was probably more subtle, arising from the feeling that they had already experienced spiritual resurrection. Therefore, anything physical—including the physical body and physical sin—was irrelevant (see 6:12; 10:23). Hence, the moral exhortation of 15:33-34 became necessary. In contrast to the Corinthian attitude stands Paul's willingness to be endangered every hour (v. 30), even before wild beasts in Ephesus (a figurative reference to an encounter with an angry mob, such as that described in Acts 19:23-41). Such a lifestyle only makes sense in light of the resurrection.

Much ink has been spilled in an attempt to explain Paul's seeming endorsement of the questionable practice of baptism-by-proxy (v. 29). Point out to the group that the intent, nature and beneficiaries of the practice are simply unknown today, so that the force of this additional argument for the resurrection has been lost to us. Don't let the group dwell on this, or you won't have time for the clearer and more important aspects of this passage!

Question 7. Paul compares the resurrection to plant life (vv. 36-38), fleshly beings (v. 39), and heavenly and earthly bodies (vv. 40-41). The group should not only identify each of these but also explain how they support Paul's argument for the resurrection.

"Spiritual body" (v. 44) does not mean nonmaterial but rather a body arising from heaven rather than from the dust of the earth (v. 47).

Question 8. Paul delights in describing how the very weaknesses that the Corinthians rightly accuse him of demonstrating (1 Cor 4:9-13; 2 Cor 10:1-11) will be reversed in heaven. This will be his ultimate victory over the seductive but false Corinthian position. See 1 Thessalonians 4:13-18 for a parallel description of the Lord's coming and the victorious experience to which believers can look forward.

Question 11. Paul incarnates the idea of "laboring in the Lord" in the final chapter, specifically in the context of (1) collecting funds to aid the hungry saints of povertyand famine-stricken Judea; (2) welcoming and assisting itinerant Christian workers; (3) remaining for a period of quality ministry in a region; (4) submitting to leaders and laborers in the work; and (5) sending gifts, both funds and friendship, to workers in isolated situations. Finally, the sympathetic reference to Apollos may represent the most powerful illustration of all, for it points to a spirit of unity and cooperation so lacking in the church at Corinth (see 1:12; 3:4).

Daniel G. Williams is pastor of New Life Community Church in Burnaby, British Columbia. R. Paul Stevens is professor emeritus of marketplace theology and leadership at Regent College, Vancouver, British Columbia.